BECOMING

THE STORY OF GRACE AFTER THE FALL

The Story of Grace After the Fall

"The light shines in the darkness, and the darkness did not comprehend it."—John 1:5 (NKJV)

Latoya Shea

Let There Be Light Publishing

COPYRIGHT

DEDICATION

For everyone who thought their story was over. May you come to see that God's grace never ends, and His light never truly leaves.Even in the silence, He is writing your becoming.

Dedicated to every believer rebuilding after the fall. May this story remind you that grace is not just forgiveness; it's the power to rise again, to become all that God called you to be, page by page, prayer by prayer.

ACKNOWLEDGMENTS

To my **Heavenly Father**, my first love, my anchor, my rescue, my breath—every word of this story belongs to You. You carried me through fire and brought me out without the smell of smoke. Your love is the only reason I am still here. All glory be to Jesus Christ, forever and always.

To my **Grandmother**, who prayed seeds into the soil of my soul long before I understood them. Your faith fed me when food could not. Your voice still echoes in my spirit: *"The stone the builders rejected shall become the head cornerstone."*

To **Aunt Angela**, your sacrifices shaped my foundation. Your love was provision. Your prayers kept me when I did not have the strength to keep myself. Thank you for loving me before I understood the weight of love.

To **Abi**, my sweet girl—thank you for standing with me in the darkest nights. Your hands, your prayers, your presence were a lifeline. God saw you. God remembers. Nothing you did in love will ever be forgotten.

To **Tabitha** and **Stacy**, my sisters in the Spirit—thank you for fasting when I could not fast, praying when I could not pray, speaking life when the valley was too deep. You helped me remember who I was when the enemy tried to erase me.

To **Brian**, my love. Thank you for the times that you were there and the great memories we shared. You were a first for me in many ways that I never expressed. I know God's plans are perfect. May they prevail in your life always.

To **Ellen**, your kindness was light. In a season where many turned away, your calls, your prayers, your gentle encouragement reminded me that God always preserves a remnant of love.

To **Ryan, Deanna** and **Josh**, who showed up when I could not stand, who carried faith when mine was faltering, and who reminded me that God often sends help through obedience, not answers. Thanks for your steady presence, honesty, and quiet strength that anchored me in moments when everything felt unmoored.

To **Steve**, who stayed without needing to understand everything, who walked with me through confusion and pain, and whose loyalty reflected the kind of friendship that does not disappear when life becomes costly.

To **Janice** and **Hilary**, thank you for the prayer sessions and the words of encouragement that helped me to keep going when everything in me tried to stop.

To **Elizabeth** and **Sarah**, you stood faithfully by me without even knowing that I was going through a storm. Thank you for your love and support, which were constant and very well needed.

To **Pastor Mary**, your obedience to the Holy Spirit came like water in a desert. Thank you for standing, for carrying, for believing with me, and for being a true end-time warrior.

To **Dr. Smith**, thank you for helping me return to myself. Your counsel restored alignment when I needed grounding and strength, and your sense of humor definitely made the process smoother.

To **those who knew me** before the fire, and those who met me in it. Though unnamed, you will always hold a place in my heart. You saw the unraveling and did not turn away. You carried me when the cost became real and I could not carry myself. Whether you spoke often or stood silently, God used you to remind me I was not alone.

To **every reader**, may this testimony awaken the truth that your story is not over. No matter how deep the valley or how long the night, **God does not leave His own.** You are seen. You are held. You are loved. And your becoming is already unfolding.

Finally, to the precious **Holy Spirit**, who whispered every line—thank You. May this book do only what You send it to do.

Soli Deo Gloria — Glory to God Alone.

CRISIS, COMFORT, AND SUPPORT

IF YOU'RE IN CRISIS RIGHT NOW

●●●   If you are having thoughts of harming yourself, feeling detached from reality, experiencing overwhelming despair, or sensing dangerous thoughts telling you that you're better off gone: Pause. Breathe. Know that you are not alone. You are not crazy. You are not beyond God.

Please reach out right now to:

A trusted friend or family member

A pastor or spiritual mentor

A licensed therapist or counselor

Email me at: ***boldlybecomingbygrace@gmail.com***

Emergency services if you are in immediate danger

There is no shame in needing help. Deliverance and therapy are not enemies; both are gifts made available to you. You matter too deeply to suffer in silence.

CONTENTS

READER ENTRY PATHS

This book is a journey, but not everyone arrives to the pages from the same place. Start where your own story hurts or hopes the most.

Where to Start If...

If you are wrestling with shame from sexual sin...

Begin with Chapters 4–6, then read Selah Moment.

Let the honesty of the fall lead you into your own healing.

If you are in spiritual warfare or unexplained torment...

Start with Chapters 7–9.

You will find language for what you've been afraid to say out loud.

If you feel numb or far from God...

Begin with Chapters 10–11, especially the moments where God's whisper returns.

If you are experiencing church hurt or betrayal...

Begin with Chapters 2–3, then move to the wilderness section.

If you hunger for purpose or calling...

Start with Part I — Dreamers & Deliverers, then read straight through.

If you are reading to support someone you love...

Start with Chapter 7 and the end-of-chapter reflections.

It will teach you how to hold someone walking through the valley.

If you need help with how to wield your weapons of warfare...

Begin with chapters 12-14, then continue to the end to be encouraged.

However you enter, I pray you do not leave the same way.

SECTION 1

DREAMERS & DELIVERERS

There are seasons in life when God plants a dream inside you long before you have the strength, language, or understanding to carry it. These dreams are not fantasies; they are fingerprints. Evidence of a future Heaven has already seen.

Every deliverer begins as a dreamer.

Before purpose becomes mission, it begins as a whisper, an encounter in the quiet, a stirring no one else notices, a moment you cannot explain yet cannot forget.

This section captures the early awakenings of calling:

The visions, the promises, the gentle disruptions that signal Heaven's hand resting on your life. These are the years when destiny hides beneath ordinary days, when favor feels unfamiliar, and when God begins shaping a deliverer before they ever realize they will one day need to be one.

Dreamers are not naïve.

They are marked.

And deliverers are not self-made.

They are called.

This is where the story begins.

CHAPTER 1: THE GOD WHO SEES

"Train up a child in the way he should go. And when he is old he will not depart from it." Proverbs 22:6

I always found myself in trouble for the simple act of smiling or laughing. Even a crumpled plastic bag fluttering in the wind could send me into fits of giggles, the kind that echoed through our small home like a familiar tune. It was simply how I was wired. Joy bubbled up inside me, refusing to be stifled by the weight of the world. No matter the circumstances, I carried an unshakeable sense of contentment and security deep within me. I am Naomi Grace.

"Laughy laughy easy to lie down," my grandmother would say, her eyes twinkling with whimsy. Each time she said it, I could not help but laugh, her words wrapping around me like a gentle breeze on a sunlit afternoon. Life, however, seemed intent on stripping that joy away, throwing challenges at me like a relentless storm. Yet through every trial, I felt a quiet strength, as though He who sits in heaven was laughing with me, unmoved by the forces trying to dim my spirit.

Even before I understood what a calling was, I understood hunger. Before I learned God's voice, I learned His watching. My childhood was not gentle, but it was sacred. A place where lack became a classroom and my grandmother's prayers became the roof over every storm.

I remember mornings by the sound of footsteps moving softly through the house. My aunt Angela prepared for school quietly, careful not to wake anyone as she tied her laces. She was just a schoolgirl herself, yet each dawn she pressed a few folded bills into my palm for lunch, then began her long walk to school on an empty stomach. I did not understand then how love can deny itself so another can thrive. I only felt the warmth of her hand and the quiet assurance that God was watching us, patient as the sun rising over the hills.

Some mornings the coins stretched far enough for bun and cheese. Other days it was bulla and a small boxed milk, the sweetness fading too quickly. Abundance shifted like the tide, but love remained steady. Angela's hand would rest on my shoulder, firm and gentle, grounding me. That touch was more than comfort. It was a promise. I did not know she would go the whole day without food. I only knew she believed my future was worth the sacrifice.

I clung to Angela when she returned home, calling her name so often she would laugh and ask me to stop. She stood just shy of five feet, like my grandmother, but where my grandmother spoke sparingly, her words edged with discipline and ancient wisdom, Angela spoke softly, her voice rarely rising above a whisper.

Evenings followed a familiar rhythm. Schoolwork spread across the table, simple meals filled the air with warmth, and bedtime came quietly. On nights when dinner was absent, Angela echoed my grandmother's words, telling me to go to sleep and let angels feed me. She never complained. She carried her burdens with a quiet dignity that taught me more than words ever could.

Weekends brought chores. I scrubbed tile floors with a coconut brush, rushed through washing dishes, eager to reach Saturday morning cartoons. Tom and Jerry was my favorite. Hair washing Saturdays were special. Angela parted my thick hair carefully, washing one side before braiding it, then the other. Sometimes she tied the two plaits beneath my chin into a bow. Those moments felt like treasures, fleeting and sacred, stitched into the fabric of our life.

Mornings outside were crisp. Roosters argued with the rising sun. Yard dogs lifted their heads, then settled back down. Dust clung to our ankles above our socks as we walked. The scent of wood smoke mixed with fried dumplings drifting from nearby kitchens, making my stomach ache with hunger. I clutched my coins tightly and practiced my sums, learning early the discipline of silence and restraint, understanding that complaints did not change reality.

There came a year when my shoes gave out long before we could replace them. The leather wore thin, defeated by rain, sun, and growing feet. When my toes pressed painfully against the edges, I took them to my grandmother, already knowing a new pair was beyond reach.

She examined the shoe in her weathered hands, then reached for the old kitchen knife. Carefully, she sliced the back open just enough for my heel to breathe. "Go, chile," she said, smoothing my hair. "Walk good. God going go before you."

I walked to school with my heel exposed, laughter following me down the road. I lifted my head anyway. Faith became my armor long before I had language for it. Then the school fees ran out, and uncertainty arrived in full.

My mother dreamed of sending me to a private school. The bill arrived heavy and unmoving. The term began without me, then another. For two years, I stayed home while other children learned multiplication and sang devotion songs. I was six years old and already waiting.

My grandmother refused to let my mind idle. Each day she called me to the back step as she washed clothes, sunlight warming our skin. She told stories as she worked, scrubbing garments as if erasing hardship. When I asked if I would ever return to school, she told me the world could not take away what I learned. Then she sent me for the Bible.

We learned from its pages. Reading from verses. History from genealogies. Poetry from Psalms. Strategy from Kings and Chronicles. When I struggled, she corrected me gently. When words were too big, she made me spell and enunciate them in groups. It may sound simple to some, but these very moments meant the world to me. Scripture did not sit on the page. It settled into me.

When we finished the Bible, she pulled out the textbooks of my aunt and uncles. Spanish notes. Social studies. Mathematics far beyond my grasp. I did not understand everything, but enough took root to grow.

After two years, a family friend intervened and took me to be enrolled in a primary school on the other side of town. The teachers tested me and exchanged looks of disbelief as they said I was too advanced for the class of my age. It was until years later that I could truly comprehend that God had done it.

A year later, at nine years old, I sat the national exam and earned a place at the second ranked high school in Jamaica. And again, it did not make sense to anyone. But God rarely works within logic.

Still, prayers filled our home as my grandmother's voice rose and fell like the weather. She declared God as Father to the fatherless and taught me scripture by living it. Her faith shaped me more than instruction ever could. Though I could not see that yet.

Then the dreams began. Vivid. Heavy. Warnings I could not explain. A bus robbery. An intruder in our home. Fear wrapped tight around my chest. The next day, those dreams came alive. I had no words for it then. Only the certainty that Someone knew my name.

When my grandmother's sight faded, our home unraveled. When she was taken to the nursing home, I began wandering. From relatives to friends. From rooms to couches. I learned how to belong nowhere and everywhere at once. Then danger found me. A shack in the hills. Boys watching. A stranger warning me to leave. I followed him down the hill. I never learned his name. Only that he saved my life.

I stood at a gas station for hours until a man in a white car stopped. He gave me shelter, food, and a key. No questions. No price. Just provision.

That night, I slept in safety and understood something I could not yet articulate. I was seen.

Years later, another stranger would recognize me through a photograph. Another door would open. Another country. Another chapter unfolding.

From cut shoes to crossing oceans, I was always being carried. Even when I could not see it.

Beyond the miracles, beyond the favor, there was a Father who withheld nothing just to help me see Him.

Closing Reflection: The God Who Sees

In those days, I was unaware of how love was quietly teaching me the language of God. Even in confusion, He was present, cradling me in the shadows.

Take a moment to reflect. How often do we overlook the subtle ways love reveals itself in our lives? Not every beginning arrives with visible miracles. Some unfold through ordinary faithfulness: a hand offering lunch money in the soft light of dawn, shoes altered to fit growing feet, or the unexpected safety of a gas station where a stranger hands over a room key without hesitation.

What small gifts have carried you through your own journey? How have unanswered prayers shaped your path, gently redirecting you toward growth?

Each of these moments, though easily dismissed as ordinary, can mark profound encounters with the Lord. They remind us that the deepest transformations often begin in the quietest corners of our lives. As we learn to recognize them, we discover that even in struggle, God is patiently weaving a narrative of love and purpose, inviting us to know Him more deeply.

CHAPTER 2: CALLED TO CARRY LIGHT

"You are the light of the world. A city set on a hill cannot be hidden." Matthew 5:14

Light finds you long before you understand the weight of its glow. The day I fled for my life in Jamaica, pursued by boys whose laughter masked dark intentions, I had no idea I was being guided toward purpose. God orchestrated a chain of mercy, a stranger who offered a moment of safety, a hotel owner who opened a door, and a plane that carried me away, each step whispering the same truth. You were meant to endure this.

New York is alive with a pulse that never fades, but the Bronx has its own heartbeat, sirens, bus brakes, laughter spilling from corner bodegas, and quiet stretches where the river breeze murmurs like prayer. My apartment sat in one of those serene pockets, a gated community by the water where sandy stone buildings stood as if someone once dared to dream of peace. It became my sanctuary.

When I first stepped through the door, I struggled to accept the gift. After years beneath zinc roofs, rain-soaked streets, and shoes scarred by survival, this place felt like a miracle shaped by divine hands. It was not luxury that stunned me. It was peace. Four walls that held stillness. A refuge where my soul could finally exhale. I am always awestruck at how each new home perfectly catered to the person I was becoming, with the latter place consistently outdoing the former.

Yet gratitude did not come easily. Solitude felt unfamiliar at first. I had grown used to shared rooms filled with laughter and quarrels, noise that proved I belonged somewhere. The apartment was quiet, and quiet can be loud when you have lived through too much. I invited neighborhood kids inside just to hear laughter in the rooms, then found myself spending nights at a friend's home, craving the comfort of bodies nearby. Trauma distorts belonging and can make even blessing feel unsafe.

I remember sleepless nights in my own bed, a bed meant only for me, yet the stillness felt heavy, almost suffocating. I would curl up beside my friend's children as they slept, their small presence steadying my nervous system in ways I could not explain. Eventually, I let the apartment go. I could not reconcile my discomfort with the goodness God had handed me. It took time and many attempts before I learned how to live inside His kindness.

I never pictured myself becoming a homebody. I never imagined my sanctuary would become my safe haven or that I would pour joy into home decor, accents, and the beauty of a space. I found peace in interior design, a sharp contrast to my work as a nurse anesthetist, steady hands, controlled airways, and machines that responded to touch more than words. The operating room was sacred, life balanced between beeping monitors and hushed instructions. I learned to watch closely, to sense subtle changes before anyone named them. That was training, yes. It was education, yes. But it was also discernment, a gift nurtured under my grandmother's prayers and sharpened by survival. Long before I could explain it, I had learned how to recognize shifts in heart posture, how to know when something was no longer safe, and how to move when God was guiding me toward higher ground. Each moment had been preparing me for the light I was destined to carry.

After grueling hospital shifts, I found myself drawn to church, not out of obligation, but out of hunger. I wanted connection with believers who loved Christ and cared about purpose. It did not take long before I was serving the youth, guiding them toward Jesus in a way that felt alive. We did not sit stiffly reciting doctrine like a script. We sprawled on carpet, cross-legged, sharing stories that moved between laughter and revelation. Their questions were the kind only the Holy Spirit could answer. Innocent, bold, unfiltered.

I never had to convince them God was good. They recognized His gifts faster than most adults. They would name family, friends, even clouds drifting across the sky. If you let them talk, they could list blessings until you ran out of time, their voices rising with wonder. My approach was unorthodox, but it flowed from authenticity. It was a rhythm God wrote into me. As my influence grew, whispers followed. Some saw hope. Some sensed healing. Others felt threatened, jealousy gathering beneath the surface like a storm. But I did not understand the weight of it yet. Then God spoke to me with a clarity that cut through every noise of doubt. "I will make you great."

I was asleep when the voice filled the room, firm but gentle, spoken twice as if heaven wanted to make sure I carried it. "Open your eyes so you know you are not dreaming," He said. My body responded before my mind could catch up. I sat upright, alert, awake. In that instant, I understood the truth of scripture, my sheep hear my voice and follow. It was automatic, like the closing of a heart valve, silent, precise, undeniable.

Then He said it again. "I will make you great." Not through striving. Not through approval. Not through performance. Simply because He willed it.

I woke shaken, not with fear but with recognition, questions spinning through my head. The God who walked with me on dusty roads was still with me, now moving within me, carrying me toward a destiny I could not yet measure.

That moment opened a new season, one threaded with encounters that felt both surreal and holy. One ordinary morning I walked from the living room to my bedroom when the atmosphere shifted, as if a curtain had been pulled back. I did not stumble. I did not sway. I was simply no longer there. Whether my body stayed anchored and my spirit moved, I could not tell. I only knew I stood in a wide desert where golden sand stretched endlessly under an open sky.

A voice spoke into the stillness. "Everywhere the sole of your feet tread is yours."

In an instant I was back in my room, but the weight of that moment stayed. I did not feel powerful. I felt small, like a child staring at an ocean, overwhelmed by its depth. Later I would understand that God was staking His claim in me before He asked me to claim anything beyond me. He was preparing my heart for battles ahead and strengthening me against the whispers that love and suffering cannot coexist.

There were other encounters, moments that made people look at me sideways, as if I were living inside fantasy. Like the day on the balcony with the Bible in my hand when the ink became radiant light. In the next moment, I was walking on cool azure water, and Jesus stood a few feet away, smiling at me as if to say, Keep going. Everything will be alright. The storm raged. Wind roared. But the space between us was safe, like a sanctuary inside chaos. Then I was back on the balcony, breath catching, reality rushing in. It did not feel imagined. It felt tangible. Wind on my skin. Water beneath His feet. A smile that wrapped around me like a well-worn blanket.

That was when I understood something about faith. Faith is not the absence of fear. Faith is movement in the presence of fear. It is learning to walk with pain you cannot explain. It is breathing in rooms where the air feels thin. Fear clung to me, refusing to release its grip, but faith rose up as something radical, a willingness to move forward anyway.

Faith was flying halfway across the world in obedience, even when prophets warned me of danger. Faith was waking at 3 a.m. with my heart hammering, thoughts spiraling into old terrors, and whispering into the dark, Lord, I know You are here, and You love me.

Faith was dragging myself out of bed, making tea, opening my Bible even when the words blurred and my thoughts resisted clarity. Faith was kneeling after long shifts while alarms still echoed in my ears, choosing to pray for the broken bodies and weary souls I had met, especially on days when my own prayers felt like they hit the ceiling and fell back down.

Sometimes I felt absurd, like a child walking through a haunted house determined to finish the tour. I learned to anticipate the spike of terror, the sudden cold, the shadows hiding in ordinary corners. But I also learned to recognize when darkness thinned, when grace appeared like a shaft of light on the next step. That is one of the promises of faith. As you keep stepping, fear begins to loosen, and love starts to warm what fear once ruled.

There were times I would ask questions, and God would answer through people, videos, dreams, or quiet revelations. But once, when I asked about a singer I admired, the answer came as a vision. I saw her in a dim office in a tender negotiation with someone I assumed was her producer. It was intimate, not something I should have seen, yet God allowed it. Not for gossip. Not to boast. To teach me that the Spirit sees beneath the surface.

My question had been simple. Was she one of His? Not to judge. Her song had recently become my anthem. In the vision, she stood firm, refusing to remove the name Jesus from her lyrics even when pressured to replace it with God. That glimpse filled me with joy. It reminded me that faithfulness is often quiet and costly.

Then came the night of miraculous healing, wrapped in the California twilight. It was not the first time I had witnessed God heal, but this was different, undeniably supernatural. I was in the Golden State for a conference, carried there by a hunger to understand what God was doing in and through me. Years earlier I had stumbled into Bruce Allen's teaching, hungry for knowledge, unaware that visions and dreams would soon become part of my life, and unaware there was a practicum that would require faith, not just study.

This time I was deliberate. A flyer for Translation by Faith crossed my path and stirred something inside me like purpose waking up.

About three days into the course, my phone rang in my hotel room. The news struck like lightning. One of my beloved church grandmas had suffered a stroke, sudden and devastating. The urgency pulled me to my knees. But as I rose from the bed, I saw the moon outside my window, a luminous crescent glowing softly. Abi's voice echoed in my mind, reminding me of our last conversation, her wonder at the moon's shape, her ability to notice beauty in the middle of struggle.

I stood at the bedside, heart racing. Sometimes my prayers came like a battle cry. Other times they came like silence. Tonight, the atmosphere felt tense. Just as I thought I had prayed enough and started to rise, a gentle voice urged me to stay. "Not yet." Then the question came. "How does someone get a stroke?"

"A clot in the brain," I answered, running through anatomy and physiology almost instinctively.

"Pray against that."

With renewed focus, I declared healing, envisioning restoration to a time before the clot formed. My words did not come with loudness but with quiet authority, the careful reverence of a novice surgeon approaching a sacred operation. Each time the Holy Spirit guided my intercession, there was an unspoken assurance that the answer was already accomplished. Before I rose, I asked if it was right to stand.

When I looked outside again, the moon began to descend, reversing its climb in a way that stunned me. My breath caught. Time seemed to bend. I stared, then worship rose out of me as I watched the moon move back down. Afterward, I searched scripture for a reference and found only the moment when God held the sun and the moon for Joshua. I remember thinking, How is this possible? I am not worthy. Nothing felt the same after that night. Not in church. Not in the spirit. When God moves openly, the enemy takes notice. I knew something had shifted within me and around me. As the encounters intensified, so did the shadows at the edge of my light, even before I stepped through church doors.

The hospital incident hit like a storm, but it had been building. I took a sip of coffee, and though I did not feel dizzy or heavy, dread crawled in like something foreign had entered me. It was early morning, cases ahead, the day moving like any other. She walked into my procedure room smiling and asked if I had cash for coffee from the cart downstairs. "Sure," I said, unaware of what was underneath that moment. When she returned with change and an extra cup, I thought nothing of it. She had always been awkward, asking strange questions about my address, but I dismissed it.

I had forgotten the warnings the Lord gave me in dreams over the years. He showed me tainted coffee, but I interpreted it as a brand issue. I even had a dream where a voice told me to stop eating red meat and coffee, but I brushed it off as dietary advice. Now the warning had become reality.

With urgency, I called my department chair. "I need to be relieved. I have to go home now." My legs felt heavy. Each step toward my condo felt like climbing through resistance. At the top of the stairs, I collapsed against the wall, gasping. That was when God's voice cut through the haze. Clear. Immediate. "Do this. Now." I obeyed.

Three days in bed followed, not a season of pity but a crucible of survival. Darkness pressed in, but I did not cower. It was the same oppressive presence that stalked me in college, the same darkness that waited in the hills. It had returned because the light in me had grown louder. God was not exposing my fragility. He was revealing His power.

When I returned to work, everything felt different. I began to understand what it meant to love those who despised me and pray for those who persecuted me. True light does not announce itself. It simply exists, and darkness adjusts. I never chased visibility. I only wanted to love God sincerely and share Him. But being seen carries a cost. I kept my thoughts about her locked away, heavy but unspoken. She greeted me with her deceptive glee, and I responded as if nothing had happened. I could not understand why she would want me harmed. I had been kind to her when others avoided her. She was beautiful, intelligent, and funny. Jealousy made no sense to me. Yet favor will provoke what it does not explain.

Another attack came quickly. This time it was a coworker I once trusted, someone I lent my favorite book to because I thought it would help her hear God's voice. That morning unfolded like many others. I arrived late again, a new pattern since the first incident fractured my routine. No matter how early I set my alarm, 3 a.m., 2 a.m., I still found myself racing through the doors. Odd stories began to swirl around my cases, but their significance did not register. My innocence was still intact.

You would think I would be hardened by everything I had survived. In some ways, I was. I understood pain and perseverance. But the spiritual realm still felt like an uncharted ocean. I assumed that suffering would lessen once I started walking seriously with the Lord. Instead, I realized the earlier fire had prepared me for a hotter furnace. As I turned to close my locker after changing into scrubs, she appeared smiling, holding out a badge holder she said was a gift for our department. A flicker of warning rose in me instantly, but I was on the phone and rushing. The first case of the day sets the tone, and I could already hear the supervisor's disapproval in my head. I accepted the badge clip with my left hand and hurried out.

It looked harmless, cheerful, smiling. But the moment it touched my palm, unease spread through me like cold water.

"Something feels off," I muttered to my friend on the line as I walked.

In the OR, I ended the call and folded the badge clip inside a glove, careful to keep it away from my right hand. The response felt automatic, guided by the Lord. By noon, my left hand tingled. By 3 p.m., numbness climbed up my arm, fingers cold and unfamiliar. Panic rose, but it lived beside a strange confidence that I would survive. I texted Chris, my Christian ally at work. We met in an empty room to pray.

Most believers around me were people I was leading to Christ. I did not want to burden them. But Ryan was different. He had grown in the spirit since we connected three years prior. I reached out to him too, desperate for agreement in prayer. With every plea, clarity sharpened. The hospital was not only a place of healing. It was a battleground. A crucible shaping me for something beyond my profession.

When I returned home that weekend, the tingling spread like wildfire, creeping into my shoulder and chest and threatening to invade the rest of my body. I wrestled alone with what to do. But I clung to God's promise. If He declared greatness, this could not be my end. The enemy threw thoughts at me, even ridiculous ones, maybe you will testify after losing an arm. The thought landed briefly, then drowned under God's authority until it became laughable.

Monday came with a gentle nudge. Fast today. I obeyed.

Later, the directive came again. Search for a prayer meeting.

After returning from Minnesota, I had spent hours hunting gatherings, dropping into random meetings without caring about distance. This time I searched with precision. In-person prayer meeting in the Bronx on Monday.

I found one on Meetup and called, but the host sounded scripted. "Do you want me to pray for you?" I asked, trying to reach beyond formality. Offended, she ended the call quickly. I kept searching until I found it. Bronx Tabernacle of Faith. A quick look at their website showed branches, even one in Jamaica. Confirmation rose in me like heat.

I called Chris while driving. That part of the Bronx was unfamiliar, dark, heavy. The GPS led me behind the building under flickering streetlights. "Don't go," Chris warned. I ended the call and kept moving. The Holy Spirit had brought me here. I could feel it.

As I climbed the narrow stairs, every step felt like resistance. It was as if an invisible weight pulled at my waist, trying to drag me back into the shadows. My chest tightened. Heat spread. Panic threatened. Still, I forced my body upward.

Inside, prayer unfolded like a sacred dance. People formed a circle, hands reaching, voices rising together. Faith wrapped around me like a covering. In that moment I felt chosen, not in pride, but in the quiet sense of being found. I kept returning, drawn by the gravity of community and spirit, waiting for the season to reveal itself.

As weeks passed, my prayers changed. They became less about what I wanted and more about who I was becoming. Even under pressure, God kept unveiling wonders. Nights by the river wind felt like holy whispers moving through my condo. Moonlight danced on the water like liquid silver. I would curl on the couch with my Bible open and feel His presence thick in the room.

I was not alone. The apartment became more than walls. It became a sanctuary where the invisible brushed against the tangible. Some nights, God spoke. Other nights, He simply listened as I poured out my heart. We laughed as I twirled around practicing ballerina moves or played with melodies that slipped away before I could write them down. The joy was too precious to interrupt.

But I also learned that calling attracts resistance, sometimes from people you never expected. Patrick was a lesson in that truth, a reminder that the oil of anointing will not always be recognized, celebrated, or understood.

There is a weight to being seen. A cost to answering the call. But God sees. He speaks. He guards. He reveals. The same God who woke me with the promise, "I will make you great," did not do it to give me applause. He did it to prepare me to love, to lead, to endure, to shine, and to stand against darkness.

This was only the beginning. Esther's favor did not shield her from plots, and I was beginning to understand the weight of that truth.

Reflection

Take a moment to reflect on your journey.

What special moments have you shared with the Lord? If you have not carved out that time yet, this is a good moment to plan your next encounter with Him. Picture it like a date with your Heavenly Father or a cozy brunch, whatever fits your personality. It does not need to be extravagant. He is already present, ready to meet you in the ordinary, to share in the things that bring you joy, and to walk with you through every season.

CHAPTER 3: WOLVES ON THE PULPIT

"Beware of false prophets, who come to you in sheep's clothing, but inwardly are ravenous wolves." Matthew 7:15

The pulpit can illuminate, but it can cast shadows too. The church, meant to be sanctuary, can become a labyrinth of hurt. Ministry was not only a calling for me. It became a source of scars. Still, even betrayal can serve purpose when God refuses to waste your suffering, and He never does.

I was full of excitement, ready to walk faithfully with the Lord. I left Minnesota behind, driven by hunger for something deeper, and returned to New York after my first fast. Looking back, it is almost comical how naïve I was, how little I understood about the road ahead. We often search for what we need everywhere else, only turning to God when everything collapses. That was my reality.

Five years earlier, I traveled to Ghana for Stacy's wedding. She was my best friend from nursing school, our bond forged in late nights and shared dreams. Watching her smile as she walked down the aisle was a moment I would not trade for anything, especially because it was my first glimpse of Africa. I returned home determined not to miss a single day of CRNA school, unaware that something dark had already started moving in the background.

Not long after, the color drained from my life. I had once been a top student, chosen as the Dean's representative and the diversity representative for New England. Suddenly I was floundering. I still showed up early to the library, still claimed my favorite window seat framed by trees, but when exams came, my mind went blank. Answers slipped away like sand. Conversation felt strained, charged with a pressure I could not name. Even small interactions became volatile. I remember arguing with a yellow cab driver over nothing. Favor, the thing that once seemed to rest naturally on my life, felt like it had disappeared. In its place was isolation.

Desperate, I reached for help in every direction. Stacy tried, but our conversations kept spiraling into conflict. My aunt Angela tried too, but concern alone could not restore what was breaking in me. I felt like a puzzle with pieces missing, and I did not know how to find them.

A psychologist tested me and said I was below the first percentile in cognitive scoring. Me. Naomi. The one who never struggled academically. Panic took over. I wondered if it was early-onset Alzheimer's. Then I went to a neurologist. The MRI showed a brain tumor. The words sat in the air like a sentence. Heavy. Suffocating. I could not accept it. It felt unreal, like someone was trying to punk me, and I refused to play along.

Out of options, I went to a psychiatrist, hoping for a lifeline. I wanted someone who could actually carry what I was carrying. I thought I found the right person, a psychiatrist from a popular reality show, someone I assumed would understand. Within thirty minutes, he was in tears over my childhood, showing me pictures of his family, while I sat there drowning in my own despair. I paid cash, hoping for breakthrough, and left feeling even more lost. Yet his words stayed with me. "You survived in spite of..."

Those 4 words became a temporary rope to hold on to. Months passed. Then a year. I forced myself through school, pouring every ounce into studying. Some nights I curled up in the shower, water running over my body like proof I was still alive. I tried to find joy in small things, Bikram yoga, painting meetups, anything that might spark life in me. Nothing hit like ice cream, everything but the kitchen sink and Phish Food Ben and Jerry's, a small pleasure that felt like the only reliable comfort I could reach.

Even travel did not lift the cloud. A trip to Italy ended with me making my aunt cry. Quebec brought its own chaos when a classmate broke her wrist just before residency. Moments that should have been bright kept turning into shadows. I kept pushing forward anyway, believing I would find my way back to myself somewhere inside the struggle.

What made it worse was that, not long before, everything had seemed to go in my favor. Getting into an Ivy League school felt effortless, almost unreal. Then the financial aid office told me about a program for Army veterans that would cover my entire tuition. It felt like God was winking at me, opening doors I never could have forced open. But those victories faded like a photo left in the sun, and I was left feeling like a castaway, drifting through despair.

In that darkness, I remembered something my friend once did when she was searching; she went to a psychic. I had laughed at it then. But desperation warps judgment. The enemy can stir chaos and then offer you counterfeit control, so you feel like your only option is to go deeper into the trap. Hosea 4:6 began to echo in my mind. My people perish for lack of knowledge. I did not truly understand what a psychic represented, or that consulting one was spiritual betrayal. As a child, I had laughed at Miss Cleo and her "call me now" slogan. Even with my street upbringing, I was still naïve about spiritual danger. I thought anything supernatural must be of God. My understanding was limited.

So when the psychic spoke of dark forces, said the enemy took my father, blinded my grandmother, and twisted my mother's heart against me because of a calling on my life, I believed her. Not because it was holy, but because parts of it sounded like my story. I had never even considered my calling. Maybe ignorance protected me for a season. But because her words felt familiar, I grabbed onto them.

God's grace is relentless. Even in rebellion, He pursued me. But I still made the choice. I searched online, dialed the number, and stepped into a rabbit hole of false hope. I spent what little money I had on phone psychics, chasing hollow predictions like oxygen. Night after night, I stood under the shower, trying to wash off a heaviness that was spiritual, not physical. I felt trapped, and my mind began to turn against me.

Then opportunity appeared, a position at a top national hospital in Minnesota. They treated me like a prized recruit, but truthfully, I accepted because I needed to escape New York's shadow. Months before graduation, I signed the contract, counting down the days until I could leave.

In Minnesota, I started to feel hope again. I pictured myself returning to the Naomi who could laugh, crack jokes, and breathe. God gave me a charming townhouse tucked among blossoming trees. Birds sang in the morning. One little bird even knocked on my antique front door window day after day like it knew me. Sometimes I studied for boards on the balcony and whispered for it to quiet down, and somehow it did. Small mercies like that made me believe life could still be beautiful.

But shadows crept back in.

My licensing and certification got tangled in delays. Furniture arrived in chaos on the same day as my exams, a day when I needed my mind to be clear. I had been sleeping on a deflated air mattress, rug fibers scratching my skin. I fell to my knees and cried out to God for focus, for clarity, for help. I passed the exam, but then had to wait again for the hospital board's approval. When the approval came, it felt like a victory, but just weeks before my first day I sliced my left thumb open trying to crack a green tea bottle with a butter knife. Absurd. Almost laughable, if I was not already exhausted.

I sensed God's favor as I stepped into the job, but darkness hovered at the edges. People were kind at first. Then the atmosphere shifted. I had the dream career, the steady paycheck, the freedom I thought would satisfy me, and still emptiness gnawed at me.

I remember sitting on a blue couch staring at the wall, whispering, "God, if it wasn't a sin to end my life, I would consider it. I feel so lost." A few days later, I knelt beside my bed and prayed, "Creator of everything, I hear so many voices about You, but I want to know who You truly are, so I don't blaspheme." Something shifted. I had traveled, met friends from many backgrounds, and explored their beliefs, Buddhism, Sikhism, Rastafarianism, all through curiosity more than commitment. I did not realize I was on the edge of transformation.

I started listening to Christian music on YouTube and walking trails while motivational speakers talked about light overcoming darkness. I followed advice without discernment. I lit white candles. I burned sage. I invited a woman from a candle shop and her Brazilian friend to my home for a cleansing prayer. I was desperate. Hosea 4:6 returned again, my people perish for lack of knowledge. Yet even in my confusion, God was drawing me.

In a bold move, I flew to Jamaica for a single day, longing to return to the church where I first encountered God as a child. I remembered being

12, walking into a night service in a miniskirt, not fully understanding anything, but crying through the altar call. A woman placed her hand on my shoulder and began to speak in a language that felt foreign yet familiar, and suddenly I was speaking it too. I left feeling changed and confused, like I had participated in something sacred without understanding it.

As a teenager, church faded into New Year's Eve services, the whole island worshiping together before my friends and I spilled into the streets for parties that lasted until morning.

When I returned for that one day as an adult, the December music and party energy felt familiar. But the church felt fractured. It had split. One faction met under a tent across the street from where my faith first ignited. That was my first internal warning.

That evening I met Pastor Smith and Deacon Rose. They welcomed me warmly. A friend had connected me to Pastor Smith months earlier because he knew I was searching. He prayed with me over the phone against darkness that felt unbearable. They ran a weekly soup kitchen. I watched them serve the community, kindness on display.

During one prayer, a voice whispered, "You're praying with them, and you're more powerful than they are." I brushed it off. I thought I was the one who needed help. Then the deacon admitted he was afraid of satan. I remember my heart racing. Afraid? I could not reconcile that with the God I was starting to reach for.

I returned the next morning determined to reclaim childlike faith. But the sermon turned into a 3 hour refrain, "I just want to cover my bishop," over and over like a hollow drum. I walked away numb. I flew back to Minnesota disillusioned.

That night I typed into my phone, "How can I get close to God?" Search results answered simply. Read the Bible. I wondered where to start. The

Gospel of John stood out. I grabbed the only Bible I owned, a gift from Susan nearly 10 years earlier. When I opened it, it landed on the baptism of Jesus. Something ignited. I said out loud, "I'm going to get baptized."

Then joy hit me like a wave. Not ordinary happiness. A euphoric surge that made it feel like heaven was celebrating inside me. I could not sleep. When dawn broke, I whispered, "You're going to have to help me today. I haven't slept in over 24 hours." God did. My assigned surgical area had only a handful of cases, a rarity that surprised everyone else and made perfect sense to me.

By the time I got home after 9, the joy still would not settle. I laced my running shoes and stepped into the cold. 20 below. Snow everywhere. I ran anyway. It felt like a divine welcome home. I thought of the prodigal son and realized joy is sometimes the Father's announcement that you are back in His arms.

From there, I consumed John's words like they held the secrets of the universe. Sundays found me on my knees, sometimes praying, sometimes begging for noon. Hunger came, but I welcomed it. Forgiveness followed. I released people verbally, one by one, loosening resentment that had lived in me for years.

Then, inspired by Jesus' 40-day fast, a quiet voice urged me to fast. It felt effortless. Darkness lifted without me even noticing. I cut ties with the outside world, disconnected my phone, and went almost silent for a year. I resigned from my job. I considered moving to California for a coveted position, accepted the offer letter, and watched them plan a welcome party in my honor. Then, a pull toward New York seized me. I got in the car, drove long highways, blasted music, and felt the thrill of something unseen guiding me.

Stacy was one of the first to hear. She did not know I was already on the road back while we talked. "I'm coming to take back everything that was stolen," I told her, not realizing the prophetic weight in my own mouth.

Before we hung up, she mentioned Pastor Vale, a marriage counselor I met in Ghana.

Do you remember him? She asked.

I did. He had sent group messages after returning to the States, including a video of a demon being cast out. The idea of demons terrified me. I had not committed my adult life to God then, and I wanted nothing to do with that topic. I blocked him immediately.

"He's been asking for you," Stacy said. "Can I give him your number?"

I hesitated, then agreed, thinking he had not wronged me personally. I had no idea what that decision would unlock. Soon I was standing in my new apartment, quiet, tucked in a corner with a view of the Hudson.

Pastor Vale and I began talking regularly. I told him I planned to take a 3 month break before starting my new job, yes, the one where I feared they might slip juju into my coffee. He told me about a sacred mountain where hundreds gathered daily to pray and encounter God. The moment he said it, something in me leaped.

Not long after, I boarded a flight with a backpack and raw determination. No frills. No matching outfits. Just hunger for God, wherever He was.

We climbed the mountain in darkness, trails steep, people ahead and behind, murmurs mixing with rustling leaves. The first days were packed with ritual. Mandatory church morning and night. Outside our quarters, congregants circled a spot where the founder supposedly encountered God. Something about it felt wrong. Vendors offered natural juices. I drank them, but food was secondary. I was hungry for something bread could not satisfy.

One day, rain slammed the zinc roof. Pastor Vale rushed in to cover items meant as a love gift. He threw his shirt over them. Instinct rose in me, and I replaced his shirt with my scarf, the one I had prayed in, worn and frayed. When he returned, his eyes widened. "What are you doing? You took my glory!" he snapped.

Confusion hit me. Glory? But the tension in the room sharpened, and I knew something had shifted.

He explained he had been collecting rainwater, "holy water," he called it, something people would buy when we descended. As he spoke, a voice cut through the moment, clear and chilling. "If you get married, you will never fulfill your calling."

No one else was there. Yet the weight landed like a verdict. I was so confused. A world was opening around me that I had no framework for. I had not learned yet that familiar spirits can speak too. I did not even know what familiar spirits were. The first time I heard that phrase, I thought it meant good spirits.

On the final day, a man approached and asked to prophesy over me. "No," I said quickly, but he persisted. "God says you think you've prayed enough, but you'll be praying a lot more. And read more."

Later, walking through Accra with Pastor Vale, I found myself speaking about Christlike character with a clarity that felt beyond me, as though the Holy Spirit was using my mouth. My words fell on hard ground. When I returned home, clarity struck like lightning. Pastor Vale was the shadow that had covered my life 5 years earlier. And the moment I blocked him again, that cloud returned.

My journey in the spirit had begun. I was being taught by the Holy Spirit, even while I was ministering to Pastor Vale. I did warn him to repent. But I was also eager, eager to burn with the fire I felt rising. So I sought prayer meetings at different churches. Midday services felt refreshing. Evening services felt different, threaded with things I could not explain, altars of flour and oil, frantic prayers for money, rituals that felt wrong even though I lacked language for why.

Then I met Pastor Patrick at a conference in Maryland. We exchanged pleasantries. That night he prophesied over me. It was my first time experiencing prophecy like that, and I did not know what to do with it. He was short, small in stature, but when he preached it sounded like a lion, commanding attention.

That night in my hotel room, voices pressed into my mind, insisting he was my husband. The same tone I had heard on the mountain. I rebuked it. My reverence for God's servants would not allow that kind of thinking. Still, the arrows landed, and they felt too familiar, echoing Pastor Vale's manipulation.

Despite my instincts, I drew closer to Pastor Patrick. I was captivated by his zeal and his ability to quote scripture. But pretense thins fast. When he visited my apartment, he spoke about Jesus, but his character did not reflect Christ. Dreams came with warnings. I brought them to him. He dismissed them or twisted their meaning.

Eventually, the Lord led me to his closet. Inside, among his belongings, I saw a coconut sprouting something strange. I found garments with my name on them, clothes that belonged to me, taken from my home. The shock hit so hard I froze. I did not understand what I was seeing or what to do, so I left it there. Later, I begged him to get rid of it and repent.

Like Joseph, I dreamed things I did not understand. Like Moses, I did not realize God was marking me for deliverance long before I could even spell the word. In hindsight, I should have asked God, the One who led me to it, what He wanted me to do next.

But I did not know. I was failing in knowledge while trying to survive. Hosea 4:6 rang again. My people perish for lack of knowledge.

Mini Retreat

Echoes From the Calling: Remembering Your First Calling

Before God sends you anywhere, He reveals Himself. Your story began long before you recognized His voice. In childhood whispers. In your grandmother's prayers. In miraculous provision. In prophetic dreams that did not make sense yet. Return there. Harvest what you missed. God was calling you even then.

Questions

- What childhood moment felt holy, even if you did not have language for it?

- Who first prayed for you?

- When did you first feel seen by God?

- What early wound shaped the way you see Him now?

- What lie about yourself was planted in childhood that God is uprooting now?

Activation

Write a letter to your younger self, telling her what God sees in her.

Prayer

Lord, reopen the early pages of my calling. Heal what hurt me. Bless what formed me. Reveal what You wrote before the world tried to edit my story. In Jesus' name, amen.

SECTION 11

LOVERS & LIONS

Love has a way of exposing what armor cannot hide.

It softens what was guarded.

It awakens what was buried.

And sometimes, it reshapes what we thought we understood about devotion, both to God and to another.

But love is never just love.

Not when Heaven is involved.

Not when destiny is at stake.

This section explores the collision of affection, vulnerability, spiritual warfare, and heartbreak. It is where longing meets calling, where sincerity meets temptation, and where the roar of inner battles becomes louder than the whisper of peace.

Lovers are tender, but lions are forged.

This is the part of the journey where the heart learns that even holy love must be tested, that faithfulness demands courage, and that some relationships carry both beauty and danger in the same breath.

Here, love becomes a classroom.

And heartbreak becomes a turning point.

CHAPTER 4: WHEN LOVE CALLED

"Two are better than one, because they have a good reward for their labor." Ecclesiastes 4:9

L ove crept in quietly as a whisper rather than a thunderclap. It arrived through a fleeting glance across the sanctuary, through shared laughter that danced in the air, and through prayers exchanged in the stillness of parked cars. Brian was an unexpected presence, tender and disarming, a gentle surprise that momentarily restored what life had stripped away from me.

Our first encounter was not marked by fireworks. It was an ordinary Monday night, a week after I had ascended the narrow BTOF stairwell for prayer night for the first time. The sanctuary enveloped me in its familiar embrace, dim lights casting soft shadows, the air thick with the scent of polished wood and the echoes of years of devotion absorbed by the carpet. I had come early, craving the solace of silence, my soul's preferred language.

He was the only other person present. Not fervently praying or preaching, but seated on the front pew, his face illuminated by the glow of a video call with a little boy, his son, though I did not know that yet. Laughter bubbled up, light and innocent, filling the empty space with warmth. It was unexpectedly tender, but my heart was in a different place. I sought solitude, not companionship. With a slight nod and a polite smile, I slipped past him, the leather cover of my Bible brushing against my thigh. I came to love the weight of His silence, that holy quiet where nothing is said aloud, yet my spirit is ministered to with a language deeper than words.

The following week, he stood by the bulletin board in the foyer, phone tucked away. Our eyes met, and his expression softened. "Hey," he said, his voice low and sincere. "About last time, sorry for the call. I did not mean to distract you." He rubbed his wrist, uncertainty flickering in his gaze. There was an honesty in his apology that caught me off guard. "Really, it's okay," I replied, holding his gaze. In that suspended moment, there was no dramatic spark, no grand declaration of attraction, just the quiet recognition of 2 souls finally seeing each other. A door creaked open in the stillness between us, hinting at a path yet to be traveled.

I had not sought out Brian. I had surrendered to God instead. Emerging from a wilderness period after my experience with Pastor Patrick, where manipulation masqueraded as guidance, I had dedicated my heart solely to God, not from fear or bitterness, but from a realization that those drawn close to me often changed in ways that hurt. I understood now that the enemy exploited their weaknesses to attack me. I was not looking to be seen, yet Brian's presence demanded nothing from me.

He spoke softly but carried a strength forged through survival, not bravado. Muscular, yes, with a hint of streetwise charm, but beneath that exterior was a softness, a vulnerability he rarely revealed. Others noticed too, the way his gaze lingered on me during worship or as we walked together, as if I were the sole focus in a bustling room. Friends would nudge me, whispering, "Girl, that man loves you. Look at him." Strangers exchanged knowing smiles, some even dared to comment openly. Heat surged in my chest. I felt it too. Yet what struck me most was not merely how he looked at me, but how he recognized the God within me.

On Sundays, I often could not help but shout, "Yeeees!" during worship, a spontaneous response to the truth stirring in my spirit. Later that week, as I stepped outside the church, he leaned in, a playful grin lighting up his face. "Yesss," he whispered, not mocking, but affirming. "I see you. The real you." That became our unspoken bond, a shared acknowledgment of faith every time we crossed paths. I would roll my eyes playfully in response, a small dance of understanding between us. But then I stepped back from church for a few weeks. A prophetic word had stirred my heart about my calling to bring out the daughters of Zion. This mission resonated deeply, because years earlier the Lord had told me how many were being pushed away from the church, and that I would be a vessel to guide His lost sheep back home. I approached my chairman, affectionately known as Dr. E. I knew he would not be happy. There is always a shortage of staff in our field. He would counsel me as one of his daughters whenever we worked together. During holidays, I looked forward to his thoughtful gifts of appreciation. I did not want to disappoint him. However, this was my Father's business, and nothing was off limits.

So I messaged asking if I could speak with him, heart pounding as I hit send. "Sure," he replied almost immediately. Then, as we stood at the elevator, I steadied my breath and faced him head on, no time for shrinking back. "I need to go per diem," I explained. I required time to delve into scripture regarding this mantle that the Lord was speaking about, recalling that the only time it was mentioned was in the story of Elijah and Elisha.

He hesitated, weighing my request. I knew this could tarnish their view of my work ethic. I had always strived to work as if for God, determined to excel in everything I did. "It's either I take 2 months per diem or I resign,"

I stated firmly. To my relief, he hesitantly agreed. I was excited to begin my 40-day quest, planning my calendar intently, no moment to be wasted. In our agreement, I worked only 2 days a week, which allowed me to dedicate the rest to Bible study, sermons, and worship.

One afternoon, as I wandered to the refrigerator from my bedroom, deep in conversation with the Lord, as was my habit, I said, "Lord Jesus, I want to feel You as my Friend. I know You are my Friend, but I do not feel it. I feel You as my Lord and King, but I do not feel You as my BFF, and I want to feel it." And just like that, I moved on to the next thought, unaware of the transformation that was unfolding in the spirit.

That night, while immersed in the dream world, I saw a massive, gleaming gold heavyweight champion belt encircling my waist. The cool metal pressed against my skin, and as I gazed at it, the engraved words caught my breath. "Signed, Jesus, Head of the Godhead, Friend of..." My heart surged with joy, and in that dreamscape I leaped into the air, shouting with exhilaration and dancing, eager to share this moment with those around me.

Among them was Brian, though I did not yet know him well. Why was he here, in my dream? I asked him this very question in the dream, unaware that this vision would hold prophetic significance for 2 years to come. When I returned to church, my heart raced with anticipation as I inquired about him. "The guy who says 'yesss' when I shout during worship," I described. But the answer hit me like a cold wave. "He left," they said. No explanation followed. "What?" Disbelief coursed through me, the image of that belt still vivid in my mind. "Can I have his number?" I pressed, fueled by the certainty that he would return. "I had a dream of him. He will be back. By the way, what's his name?"

I reached out to him, sharing the dream in a voice laced with hope and trepidation. We prayed together, not to manipulate fate or claim anything, but simply to invite God's will into the circumstances. I did not ask why he had left, and he did not offer an explanation. Our prayer concluded with a humble plea: "Lord, may we decrease and You increase, and only Your will be done, in Jesus' name, amen." He expressed doubt about returning, but I left it at that. I did not comment any further. I just said, "Okay." I forgot about it as months slipped by without contact until, just as I had envisioned, he walked back through the doors of the church.

From that moment, something tender began to blossom between us. On Friday nights, he joined my New Beginnings class. Whenever I spoke of my vow to dedicate myself to the Lord, he would raise his hand, a playful smile on his lips, and declare softly, "I object." Laughter would ripple through the room, but I sensed a deeper current beneath the humor, an unspoken language that our souls were already fluent in.

One ordinary day, devoid of any spiritual fanfare, he sent a text that shattered the mundane. "I am interested in you." It was simple, raw, and honest, yet it struck me like lightning. I froze, my heart racing, overwhelmed by emotions I could not quite grasp. Jericho was crumbling silently within me, and I was not prepared for this.

Weeks passed, filled with shared laughter at church functions, an easy camaraderie that felt timeless. But then, 1 Friday night, something shifted. An unfamiliar sensation washed over me, an overwhelming warmth in my chest that defied description. For the first time, I truly saw him. We had exchanged words and shared experiences, but I had never truly looked into his eyes. It was as if a veil had lifted, revealing not just the essence of who he was, but his physical appearance as well.

The following night, after another church gathering, we drove to his Harlem home. The car was wrapped in a profound silence, the kind that signals truth is about to surface. As we pulled up to his apartment, I opened up about my past, the disappointments, the manipulation, the spiritual betrayals that made me even more intent on keeping focused on the Lord.

"I guard my heart," I confessed, "because I have learned that the enemy often strikes through those closest to me. I do not want you to hurt, and I will not let anyone compromise my purpose."

In that moment, I laid bare my sacrifices. My life had been stripped down to its core, a conscious choice to remain untouchable by the enemy's schemes. All I desired was to see God's will unfold, to witness His truth saturate the earth for those willing to believe. I had once yearned for a family, for the experiences that had eluded me, but after my encounter with Pastor Patrick, I had come to realize it was not worth the risk of thwarting God's plans.

He paused, the stillness between us heavy with unspoken understanding. Then, with a quiet confidence that resonated through the air, he said, "You're talking to a priest now." His voice was neither loud nor boastful, simply assured. In that moment, I felt an unexpected safety wash over me, a feeling I had not known I was seeking. It was a safety that transcended the chaos of my past, a refuge far removed from the confusion, witchcraft, and heartbreak I had endured.

But it was different here, in Eden, a place of pure connection. And in that instant, I knew it was real.

CHAPTER 5: FLESH OF MY FLESH

"Create in me a clean heart, O God; and renew a right spirit within me." Psalm 51:10

It happened on a night filled with scripture and vulnerability, not lust. A moment where 2 hearts felt safe. A moment that changed everything. Sin is not always born from rebellion. Sometimes it is born from longing. And yet it invites consequences that neither of us were prepared for.

We lost ourselves in hours that felt like minutes, the world outside fading into a blur. While he worked, our conversations wove through the air like a secret melody, each word a note that lingered long after we hung up. As night fell, we gathered at the church or outside his apartment, sinking into my car's worn seats, the engine silent, windows cracked just enough to let the warm Harlem breeze dance with us. We shared everything, God's whispers, the weight of our childhoods, dreams that danced just out of reach, and fears too tender to voice aloud. Sometimes we began with prayer, our words rising like incense. Other times, we simply existed together in a comfortable silence that wrapped around us like a familiar blanket.

He lived in Harlem. I lived in the Bronx. And the car became our refuge, a vessel where 2 lives intertwined. Every evening, we made the pilgrimage to the corner store for coffee, a ritual that felt sacred. He would carry the steaming cup back to his father, but often, by the time it reached him, it had cooled, a testament to our time spent talking, laughing, and sometimes losing track of everything else. We found joy in those moments, reveling in the hours that slipped through our fingers like sand.

Sleep was a luxury. Some nights, he stole only 2 hours before heading to work. Once, we talked until dawn broke, the sky shifting from deep indigo to soft pastels as he showered and went straight to his shift. We were weary yet exhilarated, exhaustion mingling with the sweetness of connection. Love blossomed quietly, like a seed taking root in fertile soil, unaware of the storms that would come. In the chapel, we knelt side by side, praying for our community, for the church, and for each other. I watched him ask the Lord for my hand, his voice steady, but my heart hesitated. We often stayed in the church or wandered the streets for prayer walks, keeping our budding relationship a secret, believing it would shield us from the chaos of the world. Yet the truth shone in his eyes, betraying the depth of his feelings.

In ministry, he would redirect women who sought his attention to me, but I hesitated to do the same, feeling unprepared for this new territory. Not knowing that this would later be one of the thorns in the side of our relationship. Friends joked about his protectiveness of me, claiming he did not even want anyone to breathe near me, but I brushed it off, feeling flattered yet unsure. I had never felt this way before.

Before Brian entered my life, there was Sam, a connection born not from desire, but from shared faith, a bond forged in prayer when Brian distanced himself from the church. Sam reached out, seeking prayer, and I obliged, never imagining how quickly things would change. On my birthday, he gifted me a cup engraved with my name and a prayer, a gesture that felt more like kindness than anything deeper. But soon after, his life unraveled. One night he called, his voice trembling as he painted a picture of despair, no home, no family, nowhere to turn. Memories flooded back, my own nights spent under open skies, praying for solace. My grandmother's lessons echoed in my mind, share what you have, no matter how small. And as a soldier, I knew we never leave a battle buddy behind. So I opened my door.

What was meant to be a temporary refuge stretched into 10 months. I surrendered my bedroom to Sam, sleeping on the couch while my nieces filled the 2nd room. We established rules, boundaries, and respect, but loneliness crept in like an unwelcome guest. One day, he confessed his love, claiming God wanted us to marry. I said no, reminding him of my vow to the Lord. He accepted, or so I believed, until he sought out a pastor, trying to sway me. Confusion clouded my heart. We had become friends, and I cherished that closeness, especially since few understood my journey. I thought we were on the same path, both wanting to grow closer to God.

But then the attacks began as the enemy started to manifest his desires through him, each one more ferocious than the last. He even claimed the space God had carved for me, asserting ownership over our shared home. "This house is not yours," he shouted during one heated argument. "God gave it to me because I am His son and He loves me."

The words struck deep, echoing my own struggles against the limitations life had placed upon me. I wrestled with questions for the Lord, bewildered by how the enemy could infiltrate Sam's heart, a man who genuinely sought to please God. I cried out in anguish, begging for release from this burden, making every effort for resentment not to seep into my soul, toward Sam, toward God. Yet compassion held me captive.

Then Brian returned to the church, unaware of Sam's presence in my life, at least not at first. He cunningly extracted the truth from Sam, and when he looked at me, I saw the fragility in his gaze. He warned me, saying, "That can't be of God. He wouldn't have you sacrifice your secret space." But I dismissed him, convinced he was merely jealous, unable to see the truth behind his concern. I had been pouring my heart out to the Lord, yet silence wrapped around me like a heavy fog. It was not that I doubted Brian. He was my closest confidant. Still, the echoes of God's past revelations about my gifts and calling reverberated in my mind. I recalled moments when cruelty surrounded me, and God's command was to love fiercely, to forgive without hesitation. The last thing I wanted was to show Him that my desire to be with Brian had taken precedence over His will, if His will was for me to help Sam.

The Lord had been training me in ways that felt foreign to many. It was not about fleeting emotions or superficial values. It was about a deeper, unconditional love, agape love. Take Dave, for instance, a colleague I greeted daily. He was just another face in the hospital, yet through me, God seemed to weave connections that led others back to Him. To the untrained eye, it might have appeared as mere friendliness, but there was purpose beneath the surface.

Dave approached me one day, asking if I could lead a Bible study. At first, I thought he genuinely sought God, unaware that he was more interested in getting to know me. His friend had warned him about my authenticity, cautioning him that pursuing me would be a waste of time. Yet despite scheduling sessions, Dave often vanished, leaving me hanging. Then he would later bombard my phone with trivial questions, anything but spiritual matters.

I was not blind to his games. Years of walking closely with the Lord had sharpened my discernment. I could see the patterns before they unfolded, the cards he played laid bare. Sometimes I chose to engage, extending grace, because I understood that everyone wrestles with their own struggles.

But Dave's persistence wore on me. I had given him ample rope, yet he continued to play. Usually, I approached conversations about faith only when prompted by the Lord, particularly at work where boundaries felt sacred. But he kept pressing, pleading for guidance. One day, after another no-show, I finally blocked him, entering him into what I called the Block University.

The instant I did, he faded from my reality, an ability that I truly consider a gift. As soon as I deleted or blocked their number, they ceased to exist in my mind. Yet almost immediately, the Holy Spirit urged me to unblock him. Tears streamed down my face as I wrestled with the command, but obedience won out.

"Lord, if he reaches out again but does not show for Bible study, can I block him then?" I asked, half hoping for an affirmative, and I was overjoyed when He gave me the okay. Sure enough, that evening Dave texted, eager to set up another Bible study. I agreed, though deep down I wished he would flake out. And just as I predicted, he did, leaving me elated at the thought of reinstating him to my university.

The following day, as we passed each other in the hallway, he greeted me with his usual enthusiasm. I responded cheerfully, but as I turned away, a deafening crash echoed through the air. I spun around, my heart racing, only to find him sprawled on the floor, surrounded by concerned colleagues. That moment marked the end of his career. A stroke had stolen his vitality. I was consumed with guilt and sorrow that settled heavily within me.

Again, I recall another person I had interceded for, someone who had wronged me repeatedly, yet when I finally walked away, in less than a month their life was cut short. Just like that.

So it was not that I was making my decision in naivety or a lack of boundaries this time. It was a matter of life and death. How far would I go to ensure someone did not perish? This was the essence of the Father's will, that none should perish.

Christ, in His final moments, concerning the same people who would not stop until they succeeded in taking His life, uttered, "Father, forgive them, for they know not what they do." This is also why He instructs us to forgive endlessly. Since I cannot predict when someone's last chance would come, only God holds that knowledge; I try not to make such decisions without hearing from Him. It was not about submitting to a man. It was about something far greater. A true godly union meant following a man who is wholly surrendered to God's direction, and I longed for that connection. So, I was not rejecting Brian's wise counsel. I just was not sure at the time if that was God's will.

So I took an entire 24-hour prayer, seeking clarity. And finally, a word came afterwards. I led to inform Sam of my relationship with Brian, and that we were waiting to hear from the Lord on how to proceed. When I did, he responded with a casual "okay," but that simple acknowledgment spiraled into extravagant displays at church whenever he was around others.

Whispers began to circulate that he left impressions in my absence that we were more than just friends. Suddenly, Brian's warnings took on new weight. So I started to inquire on the status of his apartment hunt. He had said he was searching, but his spending habits and attitude made me realize that I needed to heed Brian's advice.

For a fleeting moment, hope flickered within me. But that was before dawn broke the day after my birthday. I had just returned from Jamaica, still carrying the scent of salt and sun, when Sam greeted me with unexpected news. He had moved out. My breath caught in my throat; my heart hung suspended in disbelief. Was this really happening? The sanctuary I craved was finally within reach. No more draping myself in summer robes to maintain a semblance of decency. No more restless nights spent fully clothed, yearning for comfort.

I stepped inside, and it was real. The room sparkled with cleanliness; fresh sheets lay invitingly on the bed, and his belongings were nowhere to be found. I whispered a prayer of gratitude. I was about to reclaim my space, my peace, for the first time in nearly a year.

When I shared the news with Brian during our morning call, relief washed over me like a cool breeze. But then the familiar beep interrupted our conversation. Sam's name flashed on my screen. "Answer it," Brian urged. We had promised each other transparency, a pact forged in honesty. He had warned me once that lies could fracture us beyond repair. And as someone who has been lied to by many, I was relieved that we shared that commonality.

As I switched calls, Sam's request echoed in my mind. Meet him at the park. "For what?" I wondered aloud, confusion threading through my thoughts. Brian stayed on the line, his presence a tether as I navigated through the labyrinth of the park, discovering paths I had never noticed before. "What does he want?" Brian asked, concern lacing his tone, but I was just as clueless as he was.

I arrived at the designated spot Sam instructed, a hidden oasis of water glistening beneath the sun. Then there he was, Sam clad in green, a color I adored. He positioned a small radio on the sand, and as music began to play, I felt an unsettling anticipation build. His words tumbled out, but they blurred together in a fog of disbelief as he knelt and revealed a ring nestled in a box.

"What in the world are you doing?" I blurted, my heart racing.

Before I could process his intentions, movement caught my eye. A stranger emerged, camera in hand, alongside his twin sister, both watching with eager eyes.

My anger flared. This was too much. The chaos of my recent trip, the hurricane, the power outages, the turmoil, had left me raw. And now here was Sam, presenting a scene straight out of a romantic comedy that felt painfully out of place.

"Just say yes, and if Dad says no, then I'll understand if you break it off," he implored, desperation etched across his face.

"No," I shot back, shaking my head.

Tears streamed down his cheeks as he pleaded, but I stood firm, my heart pounding with confusion and rage. We parted ways, both of us in tears, him walking ahead with his sister while I dialed Brian, my voice cracking.

"Why are you crying?" he questioned, his calmness a balm to my frayed nerves.

But then he did something unexpected. He comforted me as I explained the events of my encounter with Sam, who still had the keys to my car, a remnant of the surprise birthday dinner he had orchestrated. I did not dwell on how he would return them. I simply assumed I would not see him for a very long time. He had mentioned the night prior that he would be retreating to spend some time with the Lord, which left me even more bewildered by his sudden engagement at the park.

Later that evening, as Brian and I continued our conversation, the doorbell rang. My heart sank as I opened the door to find Sam standing there, tears streaming down his face. A whirlwind of thoughts crashed over me. What was he doing here? Was he okay? Did he plan to hurt me?

He stood at the threshold, words tumbling out in a rush, but my mind was already racing to conclusions. Denial clutched at my heart. This could not be true. The apartment was a lie. He had merely stashed his things in storage.

"Can I stay on the couch?" he asked, vulnerability etched in every line of his face.

My instincts screamed to protect myself, but fear twisted my gut. Yet instead of standing firm, I nodded, not out of righteousness, but because the little girl inside me could not bear to turn someone away who needed shelter as she once did. I had been sheltered by others in my youth, and I did not want to be the one to cast another person out. Thankfully, the Lord has since healed me from that fear. That night, however, I kept my decision from Brian, who sensed my turmoil but accepted my silence.

A week passed before I finally confessed to Brian. When I revealed the truth, I saw the light dim in his eyes, not from anger, but disappointment. He had asked me twice if Sam had returned to the house, and I told him no. It was not until my time in the wilderness that the Lord revealed my reason for doing this.

We had vowed to uphold honesty, yet here I was, shattering that promise. Brian expressed his uncertainty about recovering from the betrayal, but still I remained silent. The child within me, the one who had learned to hide her pain to avoid punishment, froze in fear. I did not recognize then that I was under siege, overwhelmed by the chaos around me.

Days of silence stretched between Brian and me, heavy and suffocating. Yet amidst the quiet, forgiveness began to weave its way back into our hearts, unspoken but palpable, or so I thought. I believed we had weathered the worst, that love had survived the storm. What I failed to grasp was that wounds linger, even when forgiven. Unless we surrender them to God, they remain, waiting for the moment we are weary enough to forget they exist.

The night we fell together was a twist of fate, uncharted and unexpected. We had not planned for this. Our intentions were pure, rooted in the familiar comfort of scripture. I had picked him up, expecting another evening of shared verses and quiet prayers at my apartment, but the air crackled with something new, something electric. As we settled onto the worn couch, I could feel the shift, an invisible line crossed where spirit yielded to flesh.

"No," I breathed, a whisper barely escaping my lips. But he gently grasped my chin, his gaze piercing through my defenses. "You are flesh of my flesh. Bone of my bone," he murmured, each word trembling with weight. Time seemed to suspend around us, and I found myself caught in that moment, teetering on the edge of surrender.

"I won't be with anyone else after you," I declared, my voice steady yet vulnerable.

His response came swiftly. "If this does not work out, I am done with relationships."

We shared a heavy silence, a pact forged in uncertainty. Something deep within me cracked open. Relief flooded in, mingling with safety and a profound surrender. For a fleeting instant, I dared to believe our love was a covenant, a divine promise. I felt God's presence, a warm embrace that set my heart at ease.

And then it happened. A moment of being fully seen, held, and chosen. Afterward, we sank into silence, the air thick with unspoken thoughts. We breathed in tandem, unsure of what emotions would surface next. Brian's guilt hit him like a wave, sharp and immediate, while I felt a different kind of weight, a sense of commitment, a bond that felt unbreakable.

Even as we knelt on my floor, opening to Psalm 51, conviction eluded me. Instead, I sensed something sacred had been stirred, something that had crossed a line without permission. Together we prayed, "Create in me a clean heart, O God," and in that moment I realized nothing would ever return to how it once was. The world outside faded, leaving only the 2 of us, intertwined in a new reality that would forever alter our paths.

CHAPTER 6: THE BREAKING

"For I am poured out like water, and all my bones are out of joint; my heart is like wax; it is melted in the midst of my bowels." Psalm 22:14

B reaking was not a single event. It was a relentless season that gnawed at the edges of my existence. One by one, the threads of my life began to fray, love, ministry, hope, even the very essence of who I was. The darkness did not just creep in. It stormed through the gates like an army ready for conquest.

After that night with Brian, the spiritual landscape shifted beneath us, imperceptibly at first. It was not loud or theatrical. It was a quiet disintegration, like a seam slowly parting in well-worn fabric. I had clung to the belief that love would be our anchor, that repentance could restore our balance. But I could not see that his love for me was too fragile, and that cracks were forming around us.

The first blow landed during a leadership meeting at church, where change was spoken of with enthusiasm until it turned sour. I disagreed with a decision that felt like a betrayal of our core values. I did not raise my voice. I did not rebel. I spoke calmly and respectfully, quoting scripture as my defense. Yet I had yet to learn that for some, leadership meetings were less about dialogue and more about conformity.

Perhaps I had learned this lesson but chose defiance instead. I remember telling the Bishop a few years earlier, when I was a new member, with unwavering conviction, that if anyone ever asked me to act against what the Lord says, I would refuse. Absolutely.

I had spent a lifetime searching for unconditional love, unaware that He was right there, waiting for me to acknowledge Him. And no person or their man-made rules would come between me and Him.

Tension crackled in the air before the meeting even began. Brian and I had engaged in deliverance ministry just days prior, and the buzz on social media was palpable. The Bishop preached about how every believer could cast out demons, as if it were an everyday occurrence. Ironically, I had not even believed that believers needed deliverance until recently. Brian had spent over a year trying to convince me of this, leading to countless scriptural debates. Then, during a 3-day fast, something shifted. I found myself finally agreeing to let him pray for me.

He arrived on the last day of the fast, ready to pray for hours. Exhaustion washed over me afterward, but that night I experienced one of my prophetic dreams that had been dormant for a few months. It was filled with revelations, not just for myself but for the church and its members. Those insights began to manifest the very next day, continuing for over a year. Still, I held onto questions that demanded scriptural clarity before I could fully embrace this new understanding of deliverance for believers. Experience, no matter how profound, should not overshadow the Word of God.

The following Sunday, as steam curled around me in the shower, I felt a nudge to organize a deliverance service for the next New Beginnings gathering. I laughed, incredulously. "Lord, You know I know nothing about deliverance, nor do I know what to believe about it."

Stepping out of the shower, I prayed for confirmation. Then I called Brian. "This is what I heard," I said, my voice steady despite the uncertainty swirling within me. He hesitated, repeatedly asking if I was sure, while I busily designed the flyer. It was my way of saying that I was stepping out in faith, a ritual I had adopted whenever I received a word from God.

Even when He confirmed that He had given me dominion over every place I stepped, I walked around the entire border of the Bronx, a feat that took 3 days. I did it not out of obligation, but as a declaration that I believed.

And in the early morning of the 3rd day, I had a dream where an angel said, "God said to tell you that He is working on your matter," and I woke to a song that became my anthem for the rest of the year, "On My Matter" by Ada Ehi. I had heard the song before in the past, but had to search by the lyrics from my dream before I realized its familiarity.

The Friday of deliverance finally arrived, but it felt different than other Fridays. Everyone arrived with a mix of anticipation and uncertainty, myself included. We began our usual worship, culminating in my anthem, "Yeshua." Then came the pivotal question that marked every New Beginnings meeting: "What is the gospel?" Laughter and thoughtful responses filled the room as each person took their turn. Then I shared my insights on salvation before passing the baton to Brian.

Our synergy was electric, as if we had been doing this together for years. He taught on deliverance, fielding questions with grace. Then the Lord moved among us, a palpable shift in the atmosphere.

I was excited about what the Lord was doing in and among us until the following Thursday when I attended Bible study. The air felt charged with something unsettling. It was a confirmation of the same shift I had sensed after the leadership meeting.

My name was not mentioned, but the pastor's words pierced through the crowd, targeting my very identity. She spoke of rebellion, of those seeking to divide the church, and people acting holier than thou. My heart raced, and I struggled to hold back tears. Sitting in the middle pew, clutching her phone that I was using for the livestream, I felt as though I might dissolve into the floor beneath me.

My dreams were unfolding before my very eyes, even the part that included Brian. Now it was all making sense. Sometimes my dreams are loaded with so many details, some symbolic and others direct, that I have yet to hone my interpretation skills.

In the dream from 2 years ago, I recall being led into a dark storm, and when I returned from it, Brian was at the threshold, wiping his feet continually as I moved past him. Little did I know that the storm today was merely the beginning.

Years spent in service, years filled with love and sacrifice, all culminated in a single moment where I became nothing more than a sermon illustration.

Even after being warned in dreams, I did not foresee this happening. Not like this.

It was only several months ago that I retired from my job so that I could do ministry. I thought it was a divine move, since I had received dreams of leaving work. However, the thing that finalized my decision was when I heard, "My Father needs me now," 1 Saturday night as I was praying over the map of the USA. As usual, I did not hesitate to display my act of faith. As I went to turn in my resignation, I heard an inward voice say, "Go to the staircase." I was in-between cases and did not really think anything of it, because the staircase was my hiding place when I wanted to escape everyone at work to spend time with the Lord.

As soon as I sat down and closed my eyes to pray, I felt the building swaying from side to side. I recognized this feeling. It was the same feeling I felt when I went to Nepal to aid with disaster relief after a devastating earthquake. I was not shaken, but held it in my heart as a profound confirmation that my move was causing a major response in heaven.

I had given myself to serving, and even more so after walking away from my job. Still, despite the challenges I faced, the church was home. Surely this is where the Lord would fulfill His promises to me, I thought.

Yet uncertain of how to respond to the recent events that had taken place, I embarked upon a fast for days, praying for guidance, but most of all that the enemy would not scatter the members and lead them away from the Lord as he did before with Brian. Brian, however, being too familiar with what had happened and the path that lay ahead, begged me not to leave the church.

"Just let it go," some members urged, their voices laced with concern. "This is not God. He would not lead you away after all your hard work." Their words felt like chains, binding me to a place that no longer welcomed my spirit. "You're operating in the spirit of offense," others insisted, but they did not know the half of it.

They could not see the shadows lurking in the dark, the heaviness that settled over me like a thick fog. To them, it was merely a sermon gone awry, but to me it was the closing of a door I had once thought would always stand open.

Brian, too, was shifting. The guilt weighed heavily on him, gnawing at his insides like a relentless tide. Though Sam had moved out, he remained in the church, strutting around with an air of confidence that felt foreign.

I could see the turmoil swirling in Brian's eyes, a silent scream trapped beneath the surface. Changes began to ripple through his life, transforming what should have been blessings into burdens. Old friends resurfaced, and new faces appeared, the kind that thrive on worldly pleasures rather than godly spiritual truths. Women approached him with bright smiles, eager to catch his attention. And me? I watched helplessly as the man

who once held my hand in prayer began to slip away, leaving conversations hanging in the air like unspoken words.

"We broke up before the fall," he said, his voice steady yet distant. "I love you, but I do not think we are meant to be together. God did not answer us." His words struck me like a stone dropped from a height I had not realized I had climbed.

I tried to remind him of the dreams we had shared; the prophecies spoken over us by those who barely knew our names. But fear had a louder voice than certainty, and it drowned out the truth. "I've been here before," he confessed. "And I refuse to enter another battle only to find out you are not the one."

He brought up the lie, the night I had hidden the truth about Sam. The fear that had festered inside me, a wound I had not known was still bleeding. "I can't recover from lies," he whispered. And in that moment, I was transported back to being 10 years old, hiding my pain behind a facade of silence, believing that safety lay in my own quietness.

I had carried this guilt for far too long, hating lies with every fiber of my being. As a child, I had lied about everything, earning slaps from my uncles whenever my aunt or grandmother was away. I can clearly remember the ritual of being picked up from school, with the dread of getting in trouble looming over me. There was a time when I understood that their intentions were rooted in protection, but as a child I was terrified, fearless yet constantly afraid of the consequences.

As I grew older, after being deceived by so many, I vowed to always embrace honesty, although my initial attempts were often unrefined. I would speak so bluntly, sharing my thoughts without a filter. But in time, the Master Builder shaped me, molding my raw edges into something more refined.

Then why did I lie to Brian? We shared everything, or so I thought. What lie of the enemy had I allowed to take root in my heart to lead me to this? Brian, however, dismissed the notion that the enemy played any part in this. "You are responsible," he insisted. Isn't it just like the devil to sow discord and make us turn against each other? Yet I know that our struggle is never against flesh and blood.

Tears streamed down my face as we sat solemnly. I apologized again, pouring out my heart, as he tried to forgive me as best he could, or so he said. I had believed that what we experienced would bring us closer together, even as we healed, but instead it exposed the things that lay beneath.

I had much to seek the Lord about, and for the first time in ages, I found myself with the time to do so after walking away from the ministry. The Bishop of BTOF had given me his blessing as he prayed and declared that he released me into God's hands.

Dreams and visions flooded my mind, all foretelling a valley filled with trials, yet promising victory in the end. With Abi leaving for the holidays, I anticipated a deeper connection with the Lord, eager to hear His voice amidst the chaos surrounding me. Nothing felt as it seemed, despite the reassurances of others. I needed divine wisdom, so I resolved to minimize communication with everyone, even Brian. Only the voice of the Lord mattered now.

1 dream haunted me as I prepared my heart for the days of respite that lay ahead, a vivid vision that struck during an afternoon nap. I had drifted off while listening to a sermon when an unsettling sensation bore its way into my right side. When I placed my hand there, I felt a cold, hard surface. Turning to investigate, I was met with a massive metallic object that seemed to descend from an unfamiliar heaven, an ominous sign of an enemy.

As I struggled to free myself from its grasp, a grotesque creature, resembling a mass of slugs, lunged at me from the shadows. We tumbled down what felt like endless steps, spiraling into a bottomless pit. It clung to me, urging me to denounce Jesus, but I fought back, my voice unwavering. "No! I will not!" I declared, clinging to my faith even as darkness threatened to consume me.

I felt myself slipping away, consciousness fading into a murky abyss. When I finally emerged, I was at the bottom of a dark chasm, ensnared by a grotesque, slimy creature that clung to me like a shadow. Panic surged through me as I struggled against its grip. It then appeared as if another period of unconsciousness had passed before awakening again. This time I was freed and swimming away from the sluggish creature. Swimming upward.

As I awoke from the dream, my heart raced with confusion. What did this mean? How could I be trapped by the enemy when I am secured in Christ? The questions spiraled in my mind like a whirlwind.

Then a flicker of memory sparked within me, an image so vivid it felt like a dream within a dream. It was as if I was nestled within Christ, yet somehow being pulled away, drifting out from His embrace. Desperation clawed at my chest as I fought to return, like a drowning person fighting to make their way above water so they can gasp for air. But the more I fought, the more the opening began to close, sealing me off from the light. I was caught between realms, the spiritual and the physical colliding in a tumultuous dance.

Understanding these mysteries was like grasping smoke. I could feel their presence but could never hold them. Was my departure from Christ a glimpse into the moment I was sent to this world, or was it the explanation I had been seeking for the meaning of John 10:9?

The realization struck me like a bolt of lightning. I am His rib, a part of Him, yet feeling so far removed. Did that slug-like creature symbolize my past, my repentance, and the journey back to the Lord? I had stopped asking others for help with interpretations of my dreams, tired of their bewildered looks or dismissive shrugs. Only a handful in my circle understood the weight of such visions.

In those moments, I longed for Brian. His gift for dream interpretation was unmatched, and I missed our deep conversations about the unseen battles we faced.

As the days went by, a prophecy echoed in my mind, one that warned of the reproach of Christ. I had been told it was not a punishment for wrongdoing, but rather a call to embrace suffering alongside Him, a promise that glory awaited on the other side. I wondered if these dreams were connected to the turmoil brewing in the church. But nothing could have prepared me for the slug-like storm that was coming.

Christmas Eve dawned, the air crisp as Abi prepared for her early flight to Jamaica. I admired her adventurous spirit as we drove to the airport, knowing that the 3 weeks ahead would be a sacred time alone with the Lord. I envisioned pouring my heart out, crying out for my Father in desperate need of His tangible presence. That first night, I unleashed a torrent of repentance, lamenting how I had prioritized ministry over my relationship with Him. Thoughts of Brian had long faded as I surrendered to the moment, acknowledging that forgiveness was already mine. Even if I had not hit rock bottom, nothing mattered more than my connection with Abba.

As I prayed and worshipped, the moon rose high after 3 a.m., casting a silver glow reminiscent of nights long past. The 2nd night mirrored the first, the Holy Spirit flowing through me like a river, joy bubbling up from deep within. But the 3rd day brought an unsettling shift. A heavy fog blanketed the sky, thick and suffocating, wrapping around the apartment like a shroud.

I felt a sudden heaviness pulling me into a slumber, a warning echoing in my mind about the dangers of dozing off before prayer. Nonetheless, what began as a brief nap morphed into deep sleep. Hours later I awoke unexpectedly, as if I was completely thrust into a spiritual confrontation.

Before me stood a male figure, ominous and imposing, as I lay helpless on the couch. I lifted my hand to declare, "In the name of Jesus," but a crushing force silenced me, squeezing the breath from my lungs. A vine then coiled around the left side of my body, the same side where I had once received that enchanted badge clip from my coworker, and the same side that bore the transient mark of a witch's scratch during a visit to Pastor Patrick.

This creature, a twisted mockery of humanity, then opened itself wide and began to unleash something dark and invasive within me. I lay helpless, watching as he opened up and released it. It was as if he was projectile vomiting into me, but it was coming from his core and not his mouth. And just like that, I lost consciousness again.

SELAH MOMENT
A PAUSE FOR THE SOUL

There are places in life where the story slows down, not because the journey has ended, but because something inside you must be acknowledged before you can continue. Shame, grief, temptation, fear, regret, all of it gathers like dust in corners of the heart we never sweep. This is that place. I know you may have automatically concluded that the fall refers to the rendezvous between Brian and me. Like most people, we think we are innocent if we do not engage in the big sins, but no, that is farthest from the truth. The fall, in fact, began the day I encountered the power of God in that church, the little girl in the miniskirt that spoke that strange language. Yes, it occurred that night after encountering Him and then denying Him, and every time that I have denied, rejected, or ignored Him since then. Just as the leaders did when He was in the earth.

Many of us are quick to judge the people in the Bible as we read it, picking the speck from their eyes whilst ignoring the log that is in ours, oblivious that most of us at some point were like those of whom it is written, "He came to His own, and His own did not receive Him." John 1:11

This Selah moment is a quiet space created where truth finally has room to speak.

I did not realize how loudly shame had been talking to me until everything fell apart. It was not shouting. Shame rarely does. It speaks in whispers, subtle, poisonous, looping itself around the mind until it convinces you that failure is your final identity. Shame tells you that what you did is who you are.

It tells you that you do not deserve to pray.

It tells you to hide, to shrink, to disappear.

It tells you that God has stepped back and folded His arms.

It tells you that you have ruined everything, and there is no reset.

But God asks the same question He asked Adam in the garden, "Who told you that?"

Who told you that you are disqualified?

Who told you your purpose expired the moment you fell?

Who told you there is no way back?

Who told you the story ends here?

Because that voice was not Him.

When I look back, I realize each time I fell; it was not the end. It was the place where God exposed the cracks I had learned to hide. It was where He revealed the places where I was leaning on people instead of Him. It was where He showed me how fragile my vision of love had been, and how easily the approval of others could pull me away from His voice. It was where He revealed the areas that needed pruning for my transformation to the next level of glory.

I did not need punishment. I needed honesty.

I did not need condemnation. I needed clarity.

I did not need to be thrown away. I needed to be found.

And that is what this Selah is for.

For you to see where you have been hiding.

For you to notice where shame has been narrating your story.

For you to finally tell the truth, not to God, He already knows, but to yourself. Selah

Questions

Sit with these. Do not rush.

Where have you allowed shame to silence your purpose?

What lie about yourself have you been agreeing with?

Whose voice have you been giving more power than God's?

What part of your heart have you been too afraid to bring into the light?

Where did the fall expose something you have been avoiding?

Be honest. Be tender with yourself. Be brave enough to tell the truth.

Prayer of Forgiveness & Renewal

Father,

I come to You with my whole heart, the parts that are strong and the parts that are trembling. You are not surprised by where I fell. You are not confused by my weakness. You do not withdraw Your love when I am imperfect. So I lay every secret place before You.

Forgive me for the moments I chose fear over trust.

Forgive me for the places where I hid instead of running to You.

Forgive me for agreeing with lies about who I am.

Forgive me for believing my fall was stronger than Your grace.

Wash me.

Restore me.

Lift the weight of shame off my shoulders.

Renew my mind.

Heal the places that broke under pressure.

Give me the courage to face the truth and the humility to rise again.

And Father, thank You.

Thank You for loving me in the middle of the mess.

Thank You for staying near when I thought I lost You.

Thank You for never letting go.

I receive Your mercy.

I step back into my identity.

I walk forward in grace.

I rise again, not in my strength, but in Yours.

In Jesus' name, Amen.

SECTION III

SHADOWS & STORMS

S ome storms arrive without warning.

Others announce themselves with whispers of dread before the clouds ever form.

But every storm, every true spiritual storm, reveals the shadows we've been living with without realizing it.

This section uncovers the hidden world behind suffering.

The warfare no one talks about.

The darkness that presses closer than breath.

The nights that reshape your understanding of God, yourself, and the very structure of reality.

These are the Job chapters of your journey, where faith is tested not by what you know, but by what you cannot see. Where the body becomes a battleground, the mind becomes a doorway, and every prayer feels like striking a match in a room without oxygen.

But storms, as violent as they are, never arrive without purpose.

They expose.

They cleanse.

They strip away every illusion of control until all that remains is your covenant with God.

This is where survival becomes revelation.

And revelation begins to rebuild you from the inside out.

CHAPTER 7: THE WILDERNESS BEGINS

"Yea, though I walk through the valley of the shadow of death, I will fear no evil; For You are with me; Your rod and Your staff, they comfort me." *Psalm 23:4*

Before the enemy ever touched my body, he stalked my silence. Before anything ever moved beneath my skin, darkness watched me, waiting for the moment my guard fell low enough for invasion. The wilderness did not announce itself. It entered quietly, threading through exhaustion, heartbreak, and spiritual vulnerability. One morning I woke and realized the line between the natural and the supernatural had ruptured, and something unholy had crossed through. This was the beginning of warfare I had never been taught to expect, a season where prayer felt impossible, breath felt borrowed, and survival itself became a form of worship.

When morning light seeped through the glass windows and door, I woke with weight. My body felt unusually heavy, as if something foreign had invaded my very being. My spirit echoed turmoil from within, but my consciousness failed to dial in clearly on the frequency of its message. I tried to cast it away, but still overwhelmed by fatigue, my prayers felt like arrows bouncing off an impenetrable wall, unable to rise beyond the confines of my own chest. This wasn't the first time I had battled in the spirit during restless nights, but this felt distinctly different.

I recited my usual morning prayer; the ritual meant to cleanse the remnants of night's grasp, but my words were thin, lacking the fire they once held. Still, I kept moving. Days later, I boarded a flight to California for the Crossover conference, expecting a fresh start. As the plane rose above the clouds, a phrase echoed in my mind: "Stand firm and see the salvation of the Lord." I fumbled for my phone and searched for the scripture, startled by my forgetfulness. I knew the message was divine because as I heard it, the word salvation felt faint in my perception, like a syllable slipping away. I couldn't believe I had forgotten a verse that used to live in my mouth. Still, I held it close, convinced the Lord was about to do something.

It was almost time for the New Year's Eve service when I landed, so I rushed to the hall, fatigue clinging to me like a shadow. Yet once I reached the hotel, a spark ignited. Prayer points surged through me as the Holy Spirit led, friends, family, even names I hadn't spoken in years rising up for intercession. By afternoon, I had poured out my heart and felt both drained and full. I sank into the bed, craving rest, and opened my Bible app.

Then my phone rang. It was Sam. A hesitation swept through me. This feels like a trap, a whisper rose in my mind. But how could I turn away from my brother after all I had prayed? Even that thought felt like bait, subtle and convincing.

"Sam, I can't answer," I said, steadying my voice. "I sense this is a trap of the enemy."

"What if it's not? What if I just need help hearing from the Lord?" he shot back.

"Oh, it is," I replied, frustration pressing through. He kept pushing, asking about his inability to hear God.

"Of course you know you have to spend quiet time with the Lord," I began.

"Dude, no one spends time with Him like I do," he interrupted.

I chuckled. "Not you being self-righteous." The playful tone turned sharp. Fast.

"Take it back. You can't speak to a child of God like that." His voice rose, frantic and shrill, and confusion twisted in my gut. I should have hung up. I should have blocked him. But I hesitated too long. The enemy seized the moment when my defenses were low. I snapped, and words poured out, laced with years of hurt and resentment. His role in my life. The sacrifices. The buried bitterness I swore I had healed. It all surfaced in that exchange.

The air shifted immediately, thickening with something ominous. I sensed something had gone terribly wrong. That phone call marked the last time we spoke, a finality that hung between us like a shroud.

As I prepared for service that night, anguish throbbed in my chest. I rarely reached those depths. It usually took a lot to push me beyond myself. But maybe that was the point. Overcoming lives beyond limits. I was only a fifteen-minute walk from the conference hall, still holding out hope for a divine encounter.

And as always, the Lord did not disappoint.

At the end of the service, the preacher called down fresh fire for those anointed to heal. The room filled with screams and falling bodies. I opened myself to receive. I waited. I stayed until the end. I felt nothing.

Back in my room just before midnight, I prepared for bed. As I wrapped my curls around the rod, a piercing heat struck the middle of my head. It was so painful I screamed, sure I had awakened the guests beside me. When the pain eased enough for thought to return, I assumed it was an aftereffect of the service. Later, sitting in an office chair across from the bed, a chill crept into the room. As I searched the spirit, I sensed something lingering by the window. Before I could fully understand, sleep overtook me. My body slumped forward, unconscious, in the chair.

It happened again the next night. And again after that.

No matter how I tried to stay alert, no matter how I prayed, the same strange pattern returned.

When it was time to fly home, I texted Brian, asking him to pick me up from the airport. I kept what I'd faced to myself. Who would understand, I thought. I told myself I would explain it to him in the car, that he would have insight. But when I landed in New York, he messaged that he couldn't come because he was still at church.

I pleaded. I told him I was scared to go home. He brushed it off, saying it wasn't wise since no one else was at home.

That was the moment I realized we had crossed a threshold. His concern had faded.

I wasn't asking for companionship. I was desperate for support. He should have known I wouldn't ask unless I truly needed it. The darkness had shaken me, and for the first time in years, fear crept back, wrapping around me like fog.

When I stepped into my apartment, unease hit me like a wave. I turned on every light. Friends used to tease me about how I loved unlit rooms, how the darkness was a canvas where moon and water could dance across the balcony doors. But tonight, dim corners made my skin crawl. The world outside buzzed with its usual noise, but inside, I craved brightness as a barrier.

Midnight loomed like a predator. With it came the familiar tide of anxiety that gripped me until dawn, ever since California. On the third night, desperation drove me to something bizarre. I taped myself to the wall with duct tape, a makeshift restraint against the terror that had haunted my sleep. For the first time in days, I overcame the overwhelming slumber, or so I thought.

But when I peeled off the tape and sank onto the couch, the wind returned. Stronger. It whispered through the cracks and curled around me like a serpent.

"Lord, please stop it. Don't let it hurt me," I cried, my voice frantic in the hollow space.

The more I begged, the more the pressure intensified, becoming a coarse sensation crawling up my leg, from ankle to thigh, like a rough hand tracing its way upward. I lost consciousness, not from tiredness, but from terror, unaware that the true horror was not outside. It was already stirring within.

Who could I tell. Who would understand. I didn't know. Words failed me. I hesitated because belief felt unlikely, and judgment felt guaranteed. I had always been the strong one, the prayer warrior, the one who carried others. Now I was floundering under the weight of my own silence. And drowning people do not reach out gracefully. They fight to stay afloat. They fight to understand what is pulling them under. So I stayed quiet, trapped in a storm I could not name, trying to decipher the tempest before it swallowed me whole.

The visitations began subtly, without the dramatic flair you hear in testimonies. They crept in with chilling coldness, an invisible presence invading the space where peace once lived. It wasn't a whisper. It was fear, sharp and sudden, like a switch flipped in the dark. A suffocating force pressed against me even when I stood, stealing breath and thought. Night after night, blackness swallowed me. I woke only after 6 a.m., trapped in a relentless cycle.

Still, I stayed silent. I had seen spiritual battles. But not like this. Not this invasive. Even among those who understood warfare, there were certain battles too unbelievable to share. So I carried it alone, praying in whispers as the sun dipped, bracing for nightfall like it was an appointment.

One morning, after another night lost to darkness, I woke trembling. My body felt alien, full, heavy, as if something was pressed against my skin from the inside. Sitting on the edge of the couch, breath hitching, I heard a thought rise with strange clarity: "Touch your head." It wasn't loud. It was insistent.

I lifted my hand and pressed my fingertips to my scalp, and froze.

Something shifted beneath my skull. Slow. Deliberate. Unmistakable.

It was not a pulse. Not a twitch. It was movement. My knees buckled. My vision blurred. I gripped the couch to steady myself, heart racing with horror and disbelief. I pressed again and felt it once more, smooth and gliding, like something navigating a familiar path beneath the bone, swimming as if my head held water.

I jerked my hand away. Panic surged. My mind scrambled for explanations, but nothing fit. Hallucinations don't push back. Delusions don't have weight. This was real.

That moment shattered the illusion of control I had clung to. It opened a door into a valley darker than any I had known. Everything I thought I understood about spiritual warfare felt small against this. This was not oppression. This was invasion.

I stood there paralyzed. Who could I call? How could I explain it? "I feel something swimming in my head." "Something moved from my legs and through my back." It sounded like madness. It would invite judgment.

They would assume mental illness before they ever considered the spirit. I wouldn't blame them. The truth felt too tangled to hand someone and expect them to hold it with care.

Even in the silence between Brian and me, I sensed he knew something was wrong. Months had passed since we shared anything meaningful. His heart had retreated while mine struggled to stay above water. But something stirred in him. Maybe he didn't understand it fully, but he understood enough to know I was not okay.

Instead of calling me, he contacted Ryan, our mutual friend from Connecticut, and relayed a message that felt urgent and distant: Naomi needs help. Something is happening in the spirit. She needs to come to the church. Brian didn't come. He sent an Uber.

No warmth. No presence. No protection. Just a ride.

I called him anyway, not expecting rescue, just needing the sound of something familiar.

"Hey, I'm at a baby shower. I'll come after," he said. A baby shower.

The weight of our fracture settled in my chest. The love I had clung to slipped through my fingers like sand. The hurt was quiet but deep, the kind that changes how you breathe.

Outside, the cold bit my skin. My body trembled, not only from temperature, but from exhaustion that had sunk into my bones. The city pulsed around me, horns, voices, life moving at full speed, but inside me there was a suffocating stillness. When I slid into the back seat, I caught my reflection in the window, swollen eyes, cracked lips, skin ashen, a stranger staring back.

As the car moved, I pressed my hands to my stomach and felt agitation inside me, twisting and writhing. It was as if whatever lived within me could sense where I was going. The nearer we got, the fiercer it became, mocking my hope for freedom.

I remembered the early days, how I used to seek wisdom from believers I thought were seasoned, leaders I approached with excitement, craving insight. More than once, I left feeling diminished, as if my experiences were childish. After another disappointment, the Lord spoke with clarity: "Stop asking others, for what I am doing has never been done before and will never be repeated."

Back then I did not know my body would become a battleground this literal. Then, I thought I understood what He meant.

The lights blurred past the window, streaks of gold, white, and red. Time stretched. Panic rose. My mind returned to a dream from my season away from BTOF, a vision of Brian carrying a tub of sorbet alongside a very pregnant Hispanic girl. I walked with them until he turned toward her at the gate, leaving me behind. At the time, I did not understand.

Later, reading my journal, I realized she was a dear sister in Christ, and Brian had committed to her as a godfather. Still, his choice that night felt impossible to process, especially when he knew I was fighting for my life.

When I finally stepped into the home church, warmth met me at the door, but Ryan's face shifted the moment he saw mine. I tried to smile, but inside I was barely holding it together. A small group gathered, believers who knew how to pray, how to contend, how to wage war. They worshipped. They laid hands. They called on Jesus with fire. I felt the presence of God. I felt the love in the room.

But whatever was inside me churned and resisted, twisting like a leviathan beneath the surface, scoffing at the idea of easy deliverance.

Deliverance is not always instant. Sometimes God parts waters inch by inch. Sometimes healing unravels slowly, like knots too tight to loosen in a single pull. When the service ended, they embraced me and invited me to stay until morning. I accepted. I had no desire to return to my empty apartment. For the first time in over a week, I felt a glimmer of safety. And yet Brian never came.

I curled up on the bed, knees drawn tight, as if posture could protect me from what raged inside. My hands trembled. Tears soaked the fabric of my shirt. Each breath felt jagged, like my lungs were fighting for air. And then the truth surfaced with cruel clarity.

Love can celebrate with you in bright rooms.

But only covenant stands with you in the shadows.

Brian, for all his earnestness and all the memories we had woven, did not stand. I tried to understand. I tried to excuse it. But the rejection was loud in the quiet. He was fighting his own battles and could not carry mine. That realization settled over me like a heavy blanket, pressing down until I felt utterly alone.

And yet, under all the terror, all the betrayal, all the despair, something flickered.

Not the hope I used to hold. Not the faith that once felt effortless. Not an epiphany.

Just God. Quietly beside me.

Not explaining. Not rushing. Not undoing the moment. Just there. Steady. Hidden. A silent anchor in my storm.

The wilderness stretched wide before me, vast and unyielding, but in that desolation, deliverance began to unfold. I could sense a shift, subtle movement beneath the surface of my anguish. I closed my eyes and let that presence settle into my bones.

And for the first time, I understood that sometimes healing begins with being seen, even when the night is still dark.

CRISIS, COMFORT, AND SUPPORT

IF YOU'RE IN CRISIS RIGHT NOW

● ● ●   If you are having thoughts of harming yourself, feeling detached from reality, experiencing overwhelming despair, or sensing dangerous thoughts telling you that you're better off gone: Pause. Breathe. Know that you are not alone. You are not crazy. You are not beyond God.

Please reach out right now to:

A trusted friend or family member

A pastor or spiritual mentor

A licensed therapist or counselor

Email me at: ***boldlybecomingbygrace@gmail.com***

Emergency services if you are in immediate danger

There is no shame in needing help. Deliverance and therapy are not enemies; both are gifts made available to you. You matter too deeply to suffer in silence.

CHAPTER 8: WHEN DEATH SPOKE AND GOD WHISPERED BACK

"I shall not die, but live, and declare the works of the LORD." Psalm 118:17

There is a moment in every battle when you believe the enemy's voice more than you believe your own strength. For me, that moment came in the stillness between two heartbeats, when the pain inside my body became so unbearable, the torment so relentless, that death felt like the only exit. Yet it was in that very space, where despair drowned out every scripture I had ever memorized, that God's whisper broke through. Not loud. Not forceful. Just present. And when death spoke, God did not shout over it. He answered with authoritative softness and silenced it.

There is a kind of torment that does not linger at the edges of the mind, but presses inward until it occupies a person's entire sense of self. Before this season, I never knew what it meant to feel pain that pressed directly against the soul. I had experienced spiritual warfare before. I had encountered resistance, jealousy, witchcraft, betrayal, things that would break some people permanently. But nothing prepared me for the intensity of what I was now living through. This was not a storm that came to shake my house. This was something determined to move inside and destroy it.

Day after day, night after night, every second, the creatures in my body moved. Sometimes with slow, sinister intelligence, and other times like Usain Bolt at the Olympics. They bit my nerves in ways that made my legs twitch involuntarily. They stung along my spine, sending shocks that made my back arch without warning. Every time I tried to do anything connected to God, they tightened around the base of my skull, as if I was being tortured, as if they were trying to suffocate the sound of His name inside me.

The first time I tried to read the Bible, something began to swim up my leg and through my body. I could feel it pass through my organs, then press against my vertebrae, releasing something volatile, like sparks from a fire inside me. That release would sting and bite as it made its way up to my head. It was unbearable.

Whenever I even thought about worshipping or praying, they responded with agitation. Twisting, pinching, pulsing, pushing against my inner walls. Even the faintest whisper of "Jesus," "Lord," "Father," or any name that pointed to God would stir them into motion. It felt like I had become the battleground for a war I did not understand. I was incapacitated for days, and sometimes weeks at a time.

I had signed up for a healing conference in Connecticut long before the new year dawned, driven by hope that felt both fragile and fervent. Healing was a grace the Lord had allowed me to share with others, yet here I was, desperately in need of it myself. As the moon hung low, casting a silvery glow on frostbitten ground, I wrestled with the decision to go. The pull was undeniable, ignited by the scriptures God had whispered to my heart, promising His purpose over my life. So I went.

Once I crossed the New York border, relief washed over me, as if I had inhaled fresh, prophetic air. For a fleeting moment, the turmoil within me faded, and I began to sing at the top of my lungs, worshipping as the miles melted away. But as the instructor began to speak about the Gospels and Jesus' healing ministry, the familiar torment returned, gnawing at my head with relentless ferocity. Ryan, Josh, and Deanna surrounded me, their prayers rising like incense, but nothing shifted. Physically, I was a wreck, yet my spirit soared, buoyed by the truth I clung to.

It had been weeks since I could read the Bible. With constant overstimulation from what was moving in my body and the distraction of pain, I could barely make it past a verse. Still, hunger for His Word gnawed at me. In the conference hall, I swayed my head in futile attempts to ease the pain, almost abandoning my binding prayers because the lack of change left me drained.

When lunchtime arrived and everyone clustered in groups, I craved solitude. I slipped into my car, shivering against the cold, and turned on the engine, letting heat seep into my bones. With "Victory Belongs to Jesus," my favorite song, on repeat, I reclined my seat and hovered between wakefulness and sleep. Then, something extraordinarily strange happened.

I felt a sensation as if an unseen hand had ripped away a heavy shackle from my head. It felt like a gate that had rusted shut for ages was suddenly flung open. Two objects seemed to fall onto my shoulders. I perceived them like a cluster of honeycomb. Anticipation bubbled in me as I opened my eyes. I could not wait to tell the others.

But when they returned, only nods and smiles met my excitement. What words could capture it. My mind was still under siege, my dreams and visions obscured, yet the Lord was teaching me other ways to hear and feel Him.

In the days that followed, my head throbbed as if layers of my very being had been peeled back, leaving raw sensitivity in their wake. I assumed this is what it might feel like after being scalped, or after a craniotomy. My thoughts scattered like startled birds. I would walk into the kitchen and forget why I came. I would sit on the sofa and lose track of time. What day is it? Did I eat? Did I speak to anyone? This fog was not simple emotional weakness or depression. It felt like spiritual disruption so profound it seeped into my physical senses. My heart would race without warning, and a cold weight pressed against my inner man, as if an invisible force was trying to crush me from the inside.

Gradually, I realized I had entered a valley darker than any I had ever walked through. I found myself in a place I never thought possible for someone who loved God. I stopped wanting to live. Admitting that as a believer felt like betrayal, especially after praying for countless souls, encouraging others through storms, and teaching young hearts to hear His voice. To say death felt like mercy was to challenge the very faith that had carried me since childhood. But I speak the truth because someone needs to hear it. Deep suffering does not always mean a lack of faith. Sometimes faith is the only reason you stay alive long enough to acknowledge your pain.

I did not want to die because I doubted God's goodness or love. I wanted to escape the prison my body had become, a battlefield with no refuge. Each time I closed my eyes, I prayed for a different reality. Lord Jesus, I need You. Please rescue me. Each morning I woke disappointed, pausing just long enough to see if the invaders had been devoured while I slept.

I even considered going to a rehab center just to be medicated out of my misery. But I knew that would also mean giving the devil full reign in my body uncontested, and that I could never willingly allow.

Nights found me curled on the living room floor, my body tightly wound, gasping for breath. The carpet scratched my cheek while the chill of hardwood seeped into my bones. "Lord, please. I'm begging You. Deliver me. I cannot do this anymore," I whispered, the weight of my cries hanging in the air. These were not moments of grand theatrics. They were quiet implosions, the kind that erode you instead of echoing.

He remained silent, yet steadfast. The enemy thought he could delay my reunion with Brian, hinder my understanding of deliverance, and obstruct our ministry, but all he did was propel me deeper into the school of the Spirit. Each moment became one-on-one training with the Lord. Joshua 1:9 later became a daily confession: "I am not afraid and I can never be dismayed. I am strong and very courageous because the Lord my God is with me in all means, all circumstances, all places where I am."

One night, a memory sliced through the darkness like lightning. "I will make you great." Those words reverberated in the stillness so vividly I felt the air tremble. It had been years since I revisited that moment, years since I had first begun to walk with God on this deeper path.

Back then, I had been sleeping in early morning quiet when a voice broke through, unlike anything I had ever known. It flowed like a river over stones, powerful, unwavering, unmistakably real. "I AM going to make you great," it declared.

Then, knowing I would need reinforcement because I would question every dream I ever had, He urged, "Open your eyes so you know you're not dreaming." My body obeyed instinctively. I sat up wide-eyed, and the voice echoed again: "I AM going to make you great."

In the present gloom, that memory surged through the fog like a lifeline thrown into turbulent waters.

Another vision rose, the desert scene. I stepped into my bedroom and the atmosphere shifted, pulling me into an infinite expanse of sand. Heat enveloped me, yet it felt sacred, not threatening. A voice resonated: "Everywhere the sole of your feet tread is yours." As it faded, I stood trembling, grappling with the weight of what I had witnessed.

Then came the memory of the day I saw Jesus on the water, laughter in His eyes, the wind tugging at me even while I remained seated. Peace wrapped around me like warmth.

And another memory pierced through, the day I prayed fervently for the woman who had suffered a stroke. I poured every ounce of myself into that prayer, and as I prayed, I watched the moon, bright and full, recede toward the horizon. It was as if time paused to acknowledge heaven was listening, then reversed in response.

These memories stitched together like fragments of light inside me. They were not nostalgia. They were covenant reminders, echoes of an agreement forged long before this storm.

He brought to mind our journal sessions from 5 years ago: "With greatness comes great responsibilities." The fog began to lift, revealing a truth I had known but could not feel. God had not abandoned me. This was not me trying to remember. This was my Lord reaching for me, reminding me. Something was trying to sever my connection to Him.

And if the enemy was battling me this fiercely, then my life carried weight. My calling was intact. My purpose still threatened darkness.

Tears streamed down my face, deep, shaking sobs that echoed the child in me, small, scared, yearning for arms that would not let go.

In that moment, I sensed Him, not as overwhelming force or blinding light, but gently. Like breath against my neck. Like a hand steadying the tremors in my soul. Like warmth settling in a dim room.

"I am here."

The voice was not outside me. It resonated within, quiet and certain. That assurance fueled my resolve.

Weeks slipped by in that fragile state. Some days, I managed to sit on the couch, having moved out of the bedroom. Other days, I lay flat, words escaping me in barely audible whispers.

After the healing conference, back at home, weak and still processing the surreal shift, a scripture rose within me: "They shall take up serpents with their hands." Not as something to preach. Not as a rallying cry. As a directive I could not ignore.

I brushed it aside at first. I was not trying to be spiritual. I only wanted to survive the next hour.

But then I felt it again, the familiar whale-like movement beneath my skull, rising along its usual path. This time, I did not pull away. I pressed my palm against my head, and my fingers grazed something solid, tangible. I began to whisper scripture, pulling, and something real emerged from my head into my hand. Not imagined. Not symbolic. Real.

I sat frozen, staring, confused as the weight of the moment settled on me. No sermon could have prepared me for this. No debate could hold the terror, the relief, the confusion, and the awe.

And as soon as it happened, another surged up my spine, racing to reclaim territory. This was not mere infestation. It was succession, an army determined to seize control of my thoughts.

For the first time in this relentless war, clarity dawned. I was not dying. I was being stretched, inch by inch. God was not turning away. He was teaching me how to fight.

My body shook as I whispered into the emptiness, "I will not die, but I will live and declare the mighty works of the Lord." My scalp throbbed, my breaths came jagged, my vision blurred, but something gleamed inside me, tiny and unsteady, yet resolute, refusing to surrender.

Even in horror, chaos, and silence, God remained present. Not loudly. Not dramatically. Faithfully. Patiently. And I understood something that could not be undone.

The wilderness was not abandonment.

It was where God was rebuilding me, and restoring my identity at a greater level.

CHAPTER 9: THE LONG ROAD BACK

"They that sow in tears shall reap in joy." Psalm 126:5

Healing did not arrive with triumph or trumpets. It began in small mercies: the sound of someone checking on me, the warmth of hands praying over me, the steady faithfulness of people who refused to let me disappear into the shadows. The road back was long, uneven, and often humiliating. I was not returning as the woman I once was, but as someone undone, undone and rebuilt. Yet in every undone place, God still took care of me: Ellen with her mother's compassion, Angela with prayers rooted in homeland strength, Stacy and Tabitha with intercession that held back the tide, and Abi with a childlike courage that carried more weight than she knew. Healing was not a moment. It was community.

It came not as I had envisioned, not with the thunderous crash of miracles or the awe of angels bursting through the ceiling, though that would have been nice. There were no flashes of lightning, no grand visions to illuminate my darkest nights, no divine rift in the heavens to answer my desperate pleas. Instead, it emerged like the first light of dawn, creeping across a weary sky that had forgotten the warmth of morning.

Many days, my body felt like a war zone, a landscape strewn with remnants of battles fought within. I could feel the turmoil inside me, a violent churn that left me clinging to walls just to stay upright. Some parts of me were determined to survive, while others felt resigned to surrender. Sleep often eluded me, leaving me curled on the couch, gasping for breath, waiting for the next wave of torment to recede. Nights blurred together as spiritual, emotional, and physical anguish collided, merging into chaos that obscured the boundaries of my identity.

Yet amid that wilderness, long stretches of parched earth where I felt abandoned except for God, something began to shift. Not a dramatic transformation. Not an instant miracle that would make sense to an outsider. It unfolded quietly through the hands and hearts of those around me. The same God who once gifted me visions and dreams was now weaving a tapestry of faithfulness, one thread at a time. People began to show up. They held space for me in my darkest moments, praying when I was too weak to voice my needs. They stayed when staying meant bearing witness to my suffering.

Abi and Aunt Angela became steady pillars in my life, their quiet strength a balm for my frayed spirit. Ellen, Brian's mother, came to my side even as he drifted away, derailed by distraction and guilt. Even from miles away, her presence was consistent, her voice an authority cutting through the fog of my despair. Earlier that year, she had told me God instructed her to take me as her daughter. At the time, I did not grasp the depth of what she meant, and I did not connect it to the promises Brian and I once shared in hushed tones.

Ellen did not come with judgment or assumptions. She did not try to fix my pain with hollow phrases. She offered presence. She called and messaged regularly, her voice a steady anchor amid my turmoil. She prayed with me when words escaped me, sending images and sermons full of scripture, reminders of God's unchanging nature. There was no rush, no impatience, only an abiding steadiness that felt like a miracle in the wilderness, even if just for a season.

Aunt Angela reached out every day, too, the same aunt who walked to school on an empty stomach so I could eat back in Jamaica. Her voice wrapped around me like home, reminding me of my roots, not only where I came from, but who I was at my core. She believed in my resilience, recalling storms I had faced and survived. Her prayers were not loud proclamations. They were quiet affirmations, steady as the earth beneath us, grounded in the strength of women who carried battles in silence and still kept moving.

Eventually, I confided in 2 friends, names God had woven into my story long before I understood their importance.

Stacy was one of them, my sister in every way but blood, and also by blood, Jesus's. She had sat beside me through nursing exams, early morning Bible studies, late-night cramming, and conversations that stripped us bare. When she learned what was happening to me, she did not flinch. She did not retreat. She dove into battle. "Pray for my sister," she told her bishop, not as a friend, but as family. With fervor born from knowing me and knowing the intricacies of my fight, she prayed. Her words lifted me when I felt too shattered to speak. Each prayer steadied something inside me, a tether that kept me from spiraling into the lies of darkness.

Then there was Tabitha, placed in my life months earlier, unknowingly preparing me for this very season. When she learned of my plight, she did not ask for details. She did not require an explanation that would make her comfortable. She said, "I'm fasting." And she did it, daily, a quiet warrior with no need for fanfare. Tabitha called each morning before work, not to ask how I was feeling; she already knew. She called to pray, to cover me, to hold the line. Through her intercession, I felt the muscle of my spirit begin to rebuild, layer by layer, as I stepped cautiously toward healing.

Janice and Hilary also supported me through steady prayer and timely words from the Lord when hope felt out of reach. They did not rush the process or minimize the pain; they listened, waited, and spoke only what God gave them. Their prayers and encouragement became anchors in moments when I could not see a way forward, reminding me that God was still present and still working, even when everything seemed lost.

But the one who bore the heaviest load was Abi.

Sweet, innocent, bright-eyed Abi came to New York expecting a vibrant life full of promise and adventure. Instead, she found herself in a war of the spirit, an uncharted battleground that was never on her map. I never meant for her to become my caregiver, to hear anguished cries in the dead of night, to witness my body thrashing as unseen forces clawed at my sanity. I never intended for her hands to tremble as they hovered over me in prayer, her own tears falling silently as she fought for my healing. Yet there she stood, unwavering.

When the pain became a relentless tide, Abi rubbed my skin with lidocaine gel, the only temporary balm for my torment, even though it left burning in its wake. We stocked supplies like soldiers preparing for a siege: gels, creams, sprays, all while knowing spiritual warfare does not heed prescriptions. Pain is pain, and survival sometimes demands desperate measures, even when the relief stings.

Worry gnawed at me. What were these chemicals doing to my body? How was this burden shaping her young mind? What kind of adulthood was being stolen from her as she stepped into the role of caretaker? But in the wilderness of suffering, survival narrows down to one thing: get through the next moment.

Abi became my lifeline. When I could not pray, she filled the silence with her own. When I could barely stand, she gripped my hand, her skinny fingers wrapping around mine with stubborn strength. When I could not lift my head, she leaned against me, her warmth reminding me I was not alone.

In those moments, she whispered scripture, soft but steady, trusting God to fill in the gaps of her understanding. Her youth was interrupted, but her spirit rose. She became Esther in our home, the one who stood in the gap. She became Aaron, holding up weary hands. She became Ruth, saying, "Where you go, I go," even when she lacked language for what she was carrying.

As days blurred into nights and each one felt swallowed by pain, something shifted in the air around me. My prophetic dreams began to return, first as faint echoes, hazy and fragmented, like trying to piece together a conversation after waking from anesthesia. It remained a battle; the creatures rushing to flood my mind to interrupt the messages of the Spirit. Gradually, the dreams sharpened, because who can hinder God from speaking to His children? When He said, "My sheep hear me," He meant it. And I believed it.

Alongside the dreams came scripture whispers, not thunder, not spectacle, but nudges that guided me like a lifeline through rough waters.

God was teaching me to listen again, not through visions that rattled my bones, but through quiet spaces I had ignored and through new, uncharted paths. He was rebuilding me, not through instant deliverance, but through the slow, holy work of perseverance. A healing forged in fire. Not plucked from flames, but shaped until it could withstand what was coming.

In the early days of my walk with Him, I was ablaze with excitement, ready to run into theology school. But He redirected me gently, "No. I will teach you." And He did.

Before the dreams erupted, He led me through the Gospel of Matthew and other texts, asking me questions that highlighted how messages were transmitted through dreams. Each time I would respond, "In a dream," and it was as if He was planting seeds for what would later unfold.

Then the dreams came, bursting into my consciousness, full of lessons wrapped in scripture. Like clockwork, the next day would bring a test. An unsuspecting soul would show up with a question, unaware they were my proctor. I would come home each evening replaying the conversation, remembering what I should have said, wishing I could rewind time. Then He would review the lesson with me, and we would move on, because another test would come again the next day.

And public prayer. I desperately needed extra lessons. But it was alright. I had the best Teacher, the only Teacher.

Over time, I realized something. Even though it felt like hell, I was getting stronger.

Then one day, without warning, I picked up a pen. My hand shook, my body protested, my head throbbed, but I wrote anyway. The words came slow at first, fragile and uncertain, then surged like lava breaking through the earth's crust. They carried heat and honesty, clarity I had not touched in months.

I did not write to relive pain. I wrote to hear God's whisper.

And in that moment, I understood that even before healing fully blanketed me, even before my mind returned to steadiness, even before the creatures ceased their torment, this book was going to be more than a testimony.

It was an assignment. A weapon. A conduit of deliverance, not only for me, but for every person who will one day sit alone in darkness, convinced they are the only one battling unseen foes. God was not simply restoring me. He was commissioning me.

The wilderness was not the end. It was the becoming, the title He gave me long before I understood what it meant.

Just as Job did not curse God. Jonah did not perish in the belly. I too was being held together by a God whose presence I could not always feel.

Mini Retreat Breathing in the Dark

Wilderness seasons do not come to kill you. They come to clarify you. God does His most intimate work when you cannot feel Him at all. Pain teaches what comfort never could.

Questions:

What is the darkest room you have ever walked through?

What lie did suffering try to teach you about God?

Where did you survive something you should not have?

What did the enemy hope to silence in you?

What has the wilderness revealed about your calling?

Activation:

Take a walk. Even if it is only 5 minutes. Whisper one sentence:

"Jesus, teach me to breathe again."

Prayer:

Lord, thank You for sitting with me in the shadows. For turning my trembling into testimony. Turning my pain into prophecy. Turning my wilderness into worship unto You. In Jesus' name, amen.

SECTION IV

WARRIORS & KINGS

E ventually, every storm ends.

Not always quickly.

Not always cleanly.

But when the winds quiet and the darkness lifts, something undeniable emerges: a different version of you. A warrior.

Not the loud kind. The steady kind.

The kind who knows what silence costs, what healing requires, and what obedience demands.

This section captures the rise: the rediscovered voice, the returning authority, the calling reclaimed with new understanding.

It is where identity is reforged, where purpose becomes posture, and where God crowns the places you once feared were ruined forever.

Kings are not appointed in palaces.

They are shaped in caves, tested in valleys, and crowned in the presence of the same enemies that once threatened them

These are the Esther, Joshua, and David years.

Years of rebuilding. Rising. Reclaiming territory that was yours all along.

This is where the story shifts from surviving... to becoming.

CHAPTER 10: WHEN HOPE LEARNED TO BREATHE AGAIN

"I would have fainted, unless I had believed to see the goodness of the Lord in the land of the living." Psalm 27:13

Before hope returns, it watches you. It waits for the moment your heart cracks open just enough for light to slip through again. The first day I heard God's voice after months of silence felt like someone striking a match inside a cave. Fragile. Flickering. Uncertain. But warm all the same.

The prophecies returned slowly, like pages turning in a forgotten book. The dreams came back. The desire to speak life again. And then God said something that startled new breath into me: host a healing event. I laughed at the impossibility, but heaven did not laugh with me. Hope was waking up, and it was hungry.

Healing did not make a grand entrance. It slipped in like dawn after a long night, gentle and unassuming, as if the universe itself held its breath. In those early days of recovery, miracles were elusive. There were no explosive revelations, no dramatic rescues, no nights that turned into roaring testimonies. Instead, healing crept in inch by painstaking inch, often invisible unless I slowed down long enough to notice it.

I learned to treasure small mercies. A stillness that lasted three breaths instead of one. A night of sleep without terror clawing at my mind. A moment where I whispered the name of Jesus and felt past my skin into the spirit realm again. These sparks felt insignificant, but in a barren wilderness, even embers matter.

Victory had to be redefined. It was no longer about what I was shedding but about what God was restoring. The first thing He rebuilt was not my confidence, strength, or even my physical body. It was my spiritual ear. My ability to hear Him again. The whispers. The nudges. The quiet movements of the Holy Spirit that once guided me so intimately.

That restoration began gently, through impressions rather than declarations. Subtle internal shifts, like a quiet tap on my spirit. I attended a conference in Canada, a place where I had encountered God before. Fear still followed me into the Airbnb at night, but during the daytime sessions, favor broke through in thin streams of light.

On the final day, I sat beside a volunteer I had met earlier in the conference. We bonded casually over fashion, but during guided prayer, I noticed her feet from the corner of my eye. In that ordinary moment, the Lord began to speak. Not loudly. Not dramatically. Through attention.

I have always noticed details. When something stands out, I know to ask. And when I ask, He answers. It reminded me of Moses at the burning bush. Bushes burned often on Mount Horeb. What made this one holy was not the fire but Moses' willingness to turn aside and look.

As the word unfolded, urgency filled me. When I shared what God revealed, disbelief and wonder collided in her expression. Another woman joined us, and what began as a single prophetic word turned into fellowship, prayer, and ministry as the Lord met them both.

My gifts were returning, not because I earned them back, but because grace never left. Grace does not reconsider. It remains. As I tuned back into His voice, my journal filled with scripture, dreams, and prayers. Some shaky. Some bold. Writing became as natural as breathing. My journal turned into an altar. In it, God gave me new names: Healing. Becoming. Unfinished Glory. Hope was not loud. It was steady.

Then came Pastor Mary.

She entered this chapter quietly, like healing itself. We had met years earlier in South Africa at a conference. Two women from different continents, yet when we spoke, recognition passed between us that needed no explanation. She carried authority without theatrics, precision without pride.

When I told her everything, the attacks, the torment, the creatures in my body, the nights of forced sleep, she did not flinch. She did not question my sanity. She looked at me and said, "Rise up. You are an end-time warrior."

She prayed with the ferocity of someone who understood warfare. Later, she shared the attacks that followed her prayers for me. Warfare never knocks politely. It crashes. Yet she stood firm. "The enemy does not torment what does not threaten him," she reminded me.

Then there was Steve.

Steady. Faithful. Present. He knew me before ministry scars and prophetic language shaped my world. New in his faith, he did not always have the right words, but he stayed. He prayed when asked. He listened when I could not speak. He searched scripture when I needed truth. His presence required nothing of me. Some of the holiest friendships are quiet ones.

As strength returned, the familiar pull of calling followed. Ministry had always been home. Yet fear lingered. My body still carried trauma. My mind felt fragile. I sought wisdom, not affirmation.

Dr. Smith listened without rushing. When he spoke, his words landed with weight and tenderness. "Your story is not about the attack," he said. "It is about the God who preserved you through it." He placed my suffering where it belonged, not as my identity but as testimony. "Your calling remains intact. When you serve again, you will carry resurrection in your voice."

Hope deepened.

God turned my attention back to Jesus, not the demanding version I imagined, but the One who stayed. The One who whispered instead of shouted. He reminded me of visions, of early discernment, of battles unresolved in the spirit. He showed me that innocence does not prevent warfare, but obedience equips you to survive it.

What the enemy meant for destruction, God was using for training. What was meant for evil, He was turning for good.

Hope returned quietly. In worship songs hummed under my breath. In scripture read not out of desperation but desire. In mornings without dread. In walks taken slowly, deliberately. Sometimes I prayed. Sometimes I simply breathed.

And in that breathing, I realized something holy. I was living again.

Not as who I had been before the attack, but as who I was always meant to become.

CHAPTER 11: THE CALL TO RISE

"But my horn shalt thou exalt like the horn of a unicorn: I shall be anointed with fresh oil." Psalm 92:10

There comes a point in every breaking when God stops addressing your wounds and starts addressing your identity. I felt it the morning I stepped outside and the air felt different. Not lighter. Expectant. After everything I had survived, I thought restoration would mean rest. Instead, God called me to rise. To travel. To preach. To heal. To lead. Not from the woman I had been before, but from the ashes of who I had become. Rising was not triumphant. It was obedient. And obedience became the doorway into a destiny I had nearly forfeited.

One quiet morning, the sky washed itself in muted pastels, the kind that invite contemplation rather than celebration. I stepped into the park near my home, the same place where I once shuffled along cracked pavement, whispering prayers through clenched teeth, pleading for relief from torment. This morning was different. I moved slowly, deliberately, matching my breath to my steps. Each footfall echoed with intention. I was present. I was moving. I was alive.

I began to pray, not with desperation, but with familiarity. This was no longer a cry for survival. It was a conversation. A soft exchange between two who had endured storms together and now stood in the calm. And then, quietly but clearly, the voice rose within me: "Host a healing event."

I stopped. Not abruptly, but as if a gentle hand had rested on my shoulder. I laughed, startled by the audacity of it. "Me? Now? Like this?" I whispered. "Lord, I'm not even fully healed." The impression came again. Steady. Certain. Yes. Not a suggestion. An assignment.

Fear surfaced, not from unbelief, but from reverence. I knew what warfare could do. I also knew how fragile the heart can be after battle. So I did not rush. I called my prayer partners, the ones who had witnessed my collapse and stood guard during my healing. We prayed. We waited. And when they opened their eyes, each one had received the same confirmation. It was God.

Something settled in my chest. Not relief. Surrender. God was asking me to pour while I was still healing. Like the widow who fed Elijah from her last handful of flour, I understood that God was not waiting for me to be whole before using me. He was showing me that I already was.

The call was terrifying. Humbling. Exhilarating. It felt like stepping into the reason I had been created. Like obedience was finally catching up to destiny.

My first question was simple. "Where?"

The answer came without hesitation. Not a church. This was not for the already fortified, the well dressed, or the spiritually fluent. This was for the weary. The ashamed. The bruised. The ones who would never step into a sanctuary because they did not believe they belonged. I felt God's heart beating for wilderness wanderers. Lost sheep who still recognized His voice, even while doubting their worth.

Dr. Smith spoke gently. "What about a park?"

Yes. The open air felt right. No walls. No ceilings. No barriers between heaven and the hurting. I applied for permits, filling out forms with trembling hope.

The New York permit never came through, but instead of disappointment, peace followed. The doors meant to open did. The others closed softly.

South Africa erupted with power. Healing flowed freely. Worship rose thick in the air. But Jamaica Jamaica carried weight. The moment my feet touched the island soil, I felt God ahead of me, clearing the way.

In the days before the gathering, I walked the park daily, praying, circling the track, laying everything down. One afternoon, I sat beneath a wide tree and questioned myself. Had I missed something? Had I misheard Him? And then His voice came gently, wrapping me in reassurance. You did everything right.

When the gathering came, expectancy filled the air. People arrived broken and left breathing again. Weeping turned into release. Skepticism into surrender. God moved quietly and thoroughly, like wind through wheat.

The next day, lying on the hotel bed, knees tucked, relief washing over me, I whispered, "How did I do?" His response settled over me like oil. "Well done, My good and faithful servant."

Days later, a friend texted me. "Matthew 25:23. This is how I see you and God moving." The oil had returned.

Uganda came next.

I traveled not as a recovering warrior, but as a minister reborn. Uganda greeted me with red soil, bright greens, and faces that held hardship and hope in the same breath. Children laughed barefoot, joy spilling freely. Their faith was unfiltered, instinctive.

Then Elizabeth fell.

I had met Elizabeth at a youth summer camp earlier this year before my trip to South Africa. Ryan and Deanna had invited me to volunteer while we were at the healing conference in Connecticut. I was happy I did. It was integral for me to get back to trailblazing despite the obstacles.

Elizabeth was good friends with my cabin-mate Sarah. From the first day of camp we hit it off when she started telling me about her upcoming trip to Uganda. I felt immediate confirmation, because it was less than a week earlier that Brian had message me saying that he saw that I would be focusing on the missionary part of our ministry, while he concentrated on the U.S.

Her injury cut the trip short, but something inside me also rose. Not fear. Focus. The medic in me awakened. The warrior stood. I prayed as I lifted her. I prayed through airports, wheelchairs, exhaustion, and urgency. And through it all, God stayed present.

Somewhere between prayer and fatigue, I realized it. I was standing again. Not crawling. Not gasping. Standing.

Back home, I returned to my apartment not as a survivor, but as a woman reclaiming territory. The space that once felt like a hospital room became a sanctuary. Fear no longer lived in my chest. It stood at a distance, observed but powerless.

Healing had not arrived in spectacle. It had soaked in slowly, like oil into dry cloth.

August 16, eight months after the night of the attack, marked the crossing. Joshua crossed the Jordan. And I crossed into becoming.

A Note to Pastors and Leaders

Compassion in Crisis

Dear Shepherds,

This book will land in the hands of people navigating spiritual warfare, sexual shame, mental torment, and deep confusion. Please handle them with compassion.

Not everything is rebellion.

Not every struggle is sin.

Not every torment is psychological.

Not every manifestation is demonic.

Sometimes people are simply in a fire they were never trained for.

Your gentleness may be their lifeline.

Your listening may be their healing.

Your patience may be their survival.

Lead with humility.

Counsel with discernment.

Love without assuming.

The broken do not need impressiveness. They need presence.

Just like Jesus gave us.

SECTION V

WEAPONS OF BECOMING

Joshua did not simply enter the Promised Land. He had to claim it. Step by step, territory by territory, driven not by emotion, but by obedience, discipline, and spiritual strength.

The land was promised, but it was not passive.

My journey into healing and authority reflects these Joshua years, the phase where the miracle has happened, but maturity requires partnership with God in fasting, prayer, worship, and the Word to secure what grace has given.

This section explores the practices that build a life able to hold destiny.

The fasting that starves the flesh.

The prayer that expands spiritual territory.

The Scripture that cuts through darkness.

The worship that anchors the soul.

These are the Joshua years. When victory becomes a lifestyle. When promise becomes possession. When becoming is not an event, but a way of life.

CHAPTER 12: STARVE TO LIVE

"Is this not the fast that I have chosen: To loose the bonds of wickedness, to undo the heavy burdens, to let the oppressed go free, and that you break every yoke?" Isaiah 58:6

Hunger speaks in whispers. It has a language of its own. Not merely the rumble of an empty stomach, but the low thrum beneath your ribs when your spirit longs to rise beyond the weight of flesh. Hunger hollows out what you once clung to for survival, stripping you down to pure need. And in that silence, when appetite loses its voice, something ancient begins to stir.

The first time I fasted after the attack, it was not discipline. It was desperation. A cry for something solid in the chaos. My body felt like foreign territory, unsettled and invaded. Even on calmer days, I sensed remnants of conflict beneath my skin, echoes of a war that refused to fully end. I drifted through my apartment like a ghost in my own life, present but not fully inhabiting myself.

Then came the tug. Gentle. Persistent. Not condemning. Just clear. Fast. Not as punishment. Not as penance. Just fast.

The thought terrified me. I was still fragile, still rebuilding. Fasting felt like stepping into the wilderness without armor. Yet the whisper followed me everywhere. While washing dishes. While sitting on the edge of my bed staring at the floor. Even while praying through a throat tight with uncertainty. So I surrendered.

At first, it was as easy as taking the down escalator to get to a top floor. I could barely last 5 minutes before breaking it. The psychological warfare was on the second I announced I was fasting. It's one thing to know the effects of fasting, but it's a whole other thing to have a headache and know that it's because of the octopus-like creature that has slidden between a bone.

5 minutes turned to fifteen. Then 30. Eventually, I made it from sunrise to sunset. No food. Just water. Just hunger.

The first hours passed quietly. By midday, everything shifted. The faint internal movements I had learned to fear grew louder, as if the absence of nourishment awakened shadows that had been hiding. I gripped the kitchen counter as pressure surged through my spine. Not pain. Resistance. Something realizing it was no longer being fed.

And in that moment, clarity washed over me. A verse rose without effort. Man shall not live by bread alone.

I did not speak it. I felt it.

That night, the atmosphere in my apartment changed. Sleep hovered just out of reach. At 2 a.m., I sat upright, palms pressed to my thighs, when something jolted inside me. Fear did not rise. Authority did. Quiet. Steady. Unshakeable. Fasting was not weakening me. It was weakening the darkness. Bite by bite. Squeeze by squeeze. Territory by territory. I continued. Another day. Then another.

By the third day, hunger transformed. It was no longer physical. It became an opening. Light struck differently through the living room window, as though the veil between worlds had been wiped clean.

Fasting followed a pattern. Resistance revealed presence. Presence restored power.

I would keep reading my whiteboard filled with the benefits of fasting. My favorite being that it blitzkrieg the enemy. Though not on its own. It's what's being focused on as we neglect our tummies. Anyone can starve the flesh. It's what's feeding the spirit during that time that makes all the difference.

Fasting did not make me holier, louder, or more powerful. It made me quieter. It stripped away the constant negotiation between appetite and obedience and exposed how much of my inner life had slowly grown governed by impulse rather than intention.

In the absence of food, other hungers surfaced: control, comfort, distraction, reassurance. O how often I had mistaken fullness for peace. Fasting sharpened my awareness, not by adding something spiritual to me, but by removing what dulled my sensitivity to God. I began to notice how easily I reached for substitutes when I was weary. How gently He met me when I stopped reaching altogether.

What fasting did slowly and unmistakably was reorient my strength. My body weakened, but my spirit soared. Prayer stopped feeling like effort and began to feel like alignment again. Scripture did not suddenly open with new revelations, but it settled deeper, as if it had found uncluttered ground.

Fasting did not force God's hand; nothing can. It quieted mine. In that quiet, I remembered that dependence is not a deficit but a posture. When the noise of constant consumption fades, God's presence is not louder, but clearer.

And yet another phenomenon arose. Each time I fasted, the creatures would change. It was as if I was advancing my way in a Battle Royale video game. This was a more literal take on the adage higher levels, higher devils than I expected.

The same holds true for going from glory to glory.

CHAPTER 13: WHILE MEN SLEPT

"Then He came to the disciples and found them sleeping, and said to Peter, "What! Could you not watch with Me one hour? 41 Watch and pray, lest you enter into temptation. The spirit indeed *is* willing, but the flesh *is* weak." *Matthew 26:40-41*

There comes a moment in every season of suffering when silence weighs heavier than the heart can bear. Mine broke in the stillness of night. I jolted awake, not from a dream or a sound, but from a shift in the air, the kind that makes your skin pay attention before your mind can explain it. What had felt serene now pressed against the walls, like something unseen was testing the locks on my sanctuary.

I lay frozen, heartbeat thudding in my ears like a drum. Then I felt it. A whisper, not from outside, but from deep within. Foreign. Unfamiliar. It rose the way warmth rises from coals hidden under ash, an ancient gift that had been buried beneath trauma and fear.

Tongues.

The language of the spirit. The breath of my inner man.

My throat tightened as if an invisible hand gripped it, aware of the power that was still sleeping inside me.

Not tonight, I breathed. Defiance flickered in the dark.

But the darkness pushed back. Pressure settled on my chest, heavy as lead. My limbs felt weighted. My breath turned shallow. It mirrored the silent invasion that had tried to suffocate me before. Only this time, I was awake, anchored in reality, sharpened by fasting. I could tell the difference between fear and obstruction. Something was trying to silence prayer before it formed. A thought cut through the haze, sharp and urgent.

Pray anyway.

I opened my mouth and fought for voice. At first, only ragged breaths escaped. Then a syllable cracked its way through, barely formed, barely audible. Sha. The pressure intensified, constricting like a vice. I pressed my palms into the mattress and pushed upward, as though my body needed to agree with what my spirit was trying to do.

No, I whispered fiercely. I see you.

Darkness swirled at the edges of my perception, not as a sight but as a sensation. The air thickened with intent. Another whisper rose within me, stronger now, demanding release.

Sha ra bo ko

The instant it escaped my lips, the pressure snapped. Not eased, snapped. A violent exhale tore from my lungs, like something had been thrown back, dislodged from its grip. The room shifted. The atmosphere lightened. My lungs filled with air that felt alive.

I dropped to my knees, not for drama, but because something in me needed to take the ground back with my whole body.

Then the tongues came like a torrent. Untamed. Raw. Free. They rushed from me with the ferocity of a dam breaking, years of spiritual language flooding back to reclaim territory inside my chest, my mind, my sleep. My voice grew louder, steadier, forming words I had never learned but somehow knew. A language older than my pain, older than the attack, older than fear itself.

As I prayed, my spirit expanded. I felt it stretch, as if parts of me that had been curled inward for months were finally standing upright again. Torment had trained me to shrink. Prayer made me take up space.

Jude's words pulsed through me like a drumbeat.

Building up your most holy faith, praying in the Holy Ghost.

Building. Constructing. Reclaiming.

So I enlisted prayer buddies to partner with me for time blocks. The end goal? Six hours daily.

Every syllable reinforced what the enemy had tried to fracture. Every breath erected walls, lit torches, marked boundaries. It felt like Joshua taking Jericho. Like Israel entering Canaan. The land was promised, but it had to be possessed. And it was not metaphorical, but physical.

My body. My mind. My soul. My voice. My sleep. My sanity.

Everything the enemy had trespassed was being repossessed by Heaven.

That evening, I sat cross-legged in the dim living room. Lights off. Quiet humming like a soft lullaby. I began in English, simple and honest, then shifted into tongues. It started slow, a tremor, a flutter, then deepened into something rooted. It felt like breathing underwater, except the depth held me instead of drowning me.

As I prayed, I sensed movement, not the creatures, not the old torment. Something rising within me. Capacity.

Spiritual stature.

The air shifted and a vision opened. A map.

Not of nations or cities. Of my body.

Different regions glowed faintly, chest, head, spine, stomach, hands. Some bright. Some dim. Some flickering. Some shadowed.

A voice spoke, soft and untheatrical. Territory. A glimmer over my mind. Promised land.

Then my chest lit up, steady, strong.

Mine.

I gasped and the vision broke, leaving me shaking. But I understood immediately. My body, redeemed by Christ and sealed by His Spirit, was sacred land. Promised, yes. But still contested. Just like Joshua inherited by covenant, yet still faced giants and fortified walls, I had been washed, claimed, and sanctified, yet still battling strongholds of rejection, trauma, shame, and night creatures that had overstayed their welcome.

Tongues became frontline. Each syllable felt like footsteps on holy ground.

Each breath became a boundary line. This land belongs to the Lord.

Then another truth hit me like a sober wind. In Joshua's time, some tribes did not drive out the enemy because the chariots of iron looked too strong. I realized how many believers coexist with darkness, not because they agree with it, but because they fear it. They live spiritually homeless inside their own bodies, tolerating what they were called to conquer. I had been one of them. But prayer was shifting the tide.

Not negotiation. Eviction. I prayed until my voice cracked, tears soaking my shirt, heat radiating from my spine. Then silence arrived, not emptiness, presence. Thick peace. Weighty calm. The kind that does not just comfort you, it marks you. I lay back on the floor, breath steady, heart calm.

For the first time since the attack, I sensed the enemy was no longer tracking me.

The shift was unmistakable.

I was the hunter now.

CHAPTER 14: THE SWORD THAT CUTS THROUGH THE DARKNESS

"It is the Spirit who gives life; the flesh profits nothing. The words that I speak to you are spirit, and they are life." John 6:63

In the days following that night of victory, a change began to unfurl within me. It was quiet, almost unnoticeable, yet profound. No spectacle. No loud proclamation echoing through a sanctuary. Just a gentle awakening and a sacred realization that I could inhabit my own skin again.

One morning, I opened my eyes and felt a strange lightness. My first thought was not fear. Another morning, I surfaced from sleep without the familiar terror of nightmares pulling me under. With each passing day, the weight that had pinned me down for months began to lift, as if God were fortifying my spirit from the inside out.

As I immersed myself in prayer, particularly in the Spirit, a truth took root. Prayer is not merely a survival tool. It expands you until the enemy has no room to remain

Some nights I prayed in a whisper, my voice soft in the stillness. Other nights I paced, my footsteps echoing urgency through the apartment. Then there were moments when the Spirit surged within me with such authority that even the walls felt attentive. I was not striving for power or reciting phrases meant to sound victorious. I was obeying. And in obedience, authority blossomed.

One evening, I sank to the floor with my back against the couch. My Bible rested on my lap like a warm presence. I was not ready to read. I just needed the pages near my skin, the Word close enough to breathe.

When I finally looked down, my eyes landed on a verse that stopped me.

Joshua 13:1: "There remaineth yet very much land to be possessed."

I whispered it and let it settle. Even after Jericho fell. Even after victories. Even after miracles. God still said, there is more land.

More ground to seize. More giants to silence. More strongholds to dismantle. More inheritance to embrace.

I closed the Bible with new reverence because I recognized myself in that verse. There were still places inside me that needed to be reclaimed, not because God had failed, but because healing is a possession, not a performance. There were wounds from trauma, fears that had fortified their grip, hollows carved by grief, scars that still throbbed at the touch of memory. Land waiting on the fire of the Holy Spirit.

And instead of shame, hope rose.

God was not frustrated with my pace. He was not counting my failures. He was guiding me, battle by battle, breath by breath, because this journey was never about speed. It was about transformation.

One night, a childlike question slipped from my lips.

Why tongues? Why does the enemy react so violently when I pray in the Spirit?

His answer unfurled inside me, layered and clear.

Because the enemy recognizes the language of authority, even when you do not.

That hit me like lightning without sound. The enemy was not threatened by my intellect, my voice, or my tears. He was not intimidated by my scriptural knowledge or the sermons I had preached. What unsettled him was the Holy Spirit praying through me. A prayer that bypassed every wound and every lie, traveling straight to the throne with divine precision.

The Spirit articulates the will of God.

And the will of God is the eviction notice for darkness.

That is when praying in tongues changed for me. It stopped being a spiritual discipline and became as necessary as oxygen. It felt like breathing. Like safeguarding inheritance. Like picking up a sword I did not know I had.

Around this time, a conversation with Abi etched itself into my memory.

We stood side by side at the sink, warm water washing over our hands, the clatter of plates punctuating the quiet. The window was cracked open, letting the city hum slip inside.

Auntie, she asked softly, do you think the worst is over?

I dried my hands and leaned against the counter, the weight of her question settling in my chest.

I think, I said carefully, the worst broke when I realized God did not leave.

Abi nodded, her gaze thoughtful.

And when you realized you did not lose yourself?

That pierced me. I looked at her and felt gratitude rise like a wave.

Yes, I breathed. That too.

She smiled, her eyes brightening.

I can tell. You breathe differently now.

I did not know whether to laugh or cry because she was right. Something in me was alive again. Breathing freely, fully, without bracing for impact.

A week later, while lost in prayer, the Lord stitched the threads of my season together with a single sentence.

Your spirit must grow to match the size of your calling.

Not for ego. Not for applause. For capacity. For endurance. For discernment. For weight.

Some callings are too heavy for small spirits to carry. Israel could not enter until courage matched inheritance. David could not confront Goliath until faith outweighed fear. Esther could not embrace her assignment until she endured preparation. Paul could not preach until he faced his breaking. Even Jesus fasted before confronting the enemy.

My spirit had been too thin for what God was placing in my hands.

And the warfare, as unbearable as it was, forced growth in me that comfort never could. It expanded my inner man. It rooted me in God. It strengthened what trauma tried to shrink.

It was brutal. It left scars deeper than skin. But it also revealed a truth that brought me to my knees.

The enemy attacked not because I was weak, but because he feared what God had woven into my soul.

He feared the calling that pulsed in me like a heartbeat.

He feared the anointing on my words.

He feared the authority forming in my spirit.

Most haunting of all, he feared the Christ who lived inside me, steadfast and unyielding.

Through silence, through sickness, through terror, through loneliness, through heartbreak, Christ remained. He was there in the near death moments. He was there in the confusion. He was there when I could barely whisper His name. A quiet flame in the shadows.

It did not close with a scream or a final blow. It closed with a trembling, sacred truth.

I began to believe again.

Not because I had triumphed.

Because God never abandoned the battlefield.

The wilderness lay behind me, its harshness still fresh. Healing was unfinished, like a canvas still drying. The road ahead still curved into unknown. But fear no longer held me captive in the night.

I carried fire in my bones.

And the next chapter of my life would not simply be about enduring darkness.

It would be about unleashing the light that fights back. As the Word returned to me, I unearthed an unsettling realization. The enemy recognized Scripture quicker than I did. He reacted, recoiling at the power within each verse. Each time truth rose from my spirit, my body responded, sometimes stiffening, sometimes trembling, sometimes retreating as if cornered. It became clear this battle was never truly mine. It was a clash between Him and darkness.

I was the ground where the war unfolded.

And the Word was the banner of ownership.

One morning, I perched on the edge of my bed, my Bible open but untouched. In the kitchen, Abi hummed a worship song that floated into the room like a gentle breeze. The scent of ginger tea wrapped around me, comforting yet distant. My body ached. My mind felt fragile. My spirit hovered between exhaustion and awakening.

Then I glanced down at the page, and a sentence sliced through the fog with clarity.

He sent His Word and healed them.

I traced the words with my fingers, feeling their weight.

He sent His Word.

Not a hand. Not an angel. Not a prophet. His Word.

Healing did not wait for suffering to cease. It arrived with the Word itself.

Something deep inside me exhaled, like my spirit had been holding its breath waiting for truth to become tangible.

The Word is not a tool you wield after the battle.

It is the force that enters the room before healing begins. As I spoke it, they began fleeing. Rushing for an escape.

In the weeks that followed, I discovered something startling about Scripture. When I spoke the Word aloud, my body calmed in ways no medication or breathing exercise could replicate. My heart rate slowed. Muscles loosened. Breath deepened. Vision steadied. It was as if those sacred truths pulled my nervous system out of threat mode and back into alignment. No voice brings safety like God's own.

Even when my mind struggled to grasp what I read, even when emotions were numb, Scripture bypassed every wound and spoke to the untouched place in me, my spirit. The part that belonged solely to God.

One night, the atmosphere thickened. I woke to pressure creeping along the right side of my head and fear tried to ignite. But instead of panic, something in me resisted.

No. My voice shook, hands firm, but the word held.

The pressure intensified, as if trying to choke the voice rising within me. Then a Scripture surged forth, not soft, but like a soldier storming gates.

No weapon formed against you shall prosper. It was not comfort. It was confrontation.

I sat up slowly, each movement a declaration.

No weapon formed against me shall prosper.

The air tightened, charged with tension, as if darkness listened. As if the Word entered the room ahead of me. My chest expanded. My spirit pushed back.

You cannot prosper here.

My scalp prickled. The crawling sensation stilled. And suddenly, I was no longer prey.

The Word had taken command.

I began to notice something else. Sometimes when Scripture surfaced, it came with a familiarity deeper than memory. Not the familiarity of a Sunday School lesson, but the kind that whispered, my spirit remembers Him. Verses returned exactly when needed, not because I was clever, but because He was present.

One night, in the middle of torment, a verse dropped into my mind like a stone sinking into water.

For the Word of God is living and active, sharper than any two edged sword.

Living. Active. Sharper. The Word did not just narrate the battle. It engaged.

Every time I spoke it, I was not quoting text. I was aligning with a Person.

Abi said something one afternoon that made me go still.

I was lying on the couch, nauseated, drained, the kind of tired that feels like it has weight. Abi sat beside me with her Bible open on her lap. She read quietly, brow furrowed, like she was decoding something hidden in plain sight.

After a while, she closed the book and looked at me, steady and tender.

Auntie, the Word is protecting you, even when you are too tired to grasp it.

What do you mean? I asked.

She shrugged, simple as anything.

When you cannot pray. When you cannot read. When you cannot even speak. Those scriptures you learned as a child are still fighting for you.

Her words hit me hard. Not because they were dramatic, but because they were true.

Seeds planted years ago were sprouting in the shadows.

God had built a refuge inside me before the storm ever came.

As the Word took root, shame began to loosen. Not all at once. Not with fireworks. More like morning light creeping across a floor.

The lies had been loud. You are alone.

God has abandoned you.

You are too broken now.

This is punishment.

You will never be whole again.

But the Word answered with unwavering strength.

I am with you.

My covenant I will not break.

You are Mine.

I heal the brokenhearted.

Nothing can separate you from My love.

At first, truth felt foreign, like trying on a name I had not used in years. But it lingered. It refused to fade. And slowly, it prevailed.

The Word was not only a weapon.

It was identity being rebuilt. Verse by verse. Breath by breath. Scar by scar.

The moment I recognized Scripture as a sword came unexpectedly while standing in the kitchen. The kettle hummed. Steam rose. Then that familiar pressure crept into my head, invasive and suffocating.

And a verse surged forth.

The light shines in the darkness, and the darkness has not overcome it. This time, I did not whisper.

I spoke it like a decree.

The light shines in the darkness, and the darkness has not overcome it.

The atmosphere shifted. The pressure stopped, abruptly, like it had hit a wall. My knees steadied. My breath deepened. Something retreated as if it recognized the authority of the words spoken.

That night, I learned the difference between reciting Scripture and wielding it.

Reciting reminds you of God.

Wielding reminds darkness of Him. And darkness remembers swiftly.

By the end of that week, the Word changed inside me. It was no longer external. It felt alive beneath my ribs, settled behind my sternum, pulsing through my lungs. I woke with verses on my tongue. Walked with them. Ate with them. Slept with them. Not from obligation, but because the Word had chosen to dwell within me.

And I understood something with sobering clarity.

This battle would not be won by fasting alone.

Not by prayer alone.

Not by worship alone.

It would be fought by the Spirit, the Presence, the Covenant, and the Word, together.

The sword was back in my hand.

And I was no longer afraid of the dark. I was learning to cut through it.

CHAPTER 15: BECOMING

"But as for you, you meant evil against me; but God meant it for good, in order to bring it about as it is this day, to save many people alive." Genesis 50:20

In every wilderness, there comes a moment when the dust settles. The echoes fade. The shadows loosen their grip. A breath enters your lungs that does not taste like fear.

For me, clarity came slowly, like dawn sliding over a horizon that had been dark for too long. It was not the blinding light of a miracle that erased scars. It was gentler than that. A restoration of strength. A quiet return of myself. Sacred, steady, and almost surprising.

At first, the calm was disorienting. After years of being chased by the night, waking up without dread felt almost like betrayal. I stood with legs trembling as if they belonged to someone else and then, out of nowhere, laughter bubbled up. Unpracticed. Unfamiliar. Real. It echoed in my chest like a language I had forgotten I could speak.

That was the beginning of my transformation.

Not the polished metamorphosis that looks good on book covers. Not the kind that earns applause. This was raw becoming, born from surviving what should have broken me.

I did not rise because I was strong. I rose because God's hand stayed firm on my back, even when my grip on Him faltered. There was no drama, no fanfare, no theatrical moment that made everything suddenly make sense. It was simply the steady realization that survival was not the finish line. Purpose was waiting.

I understood then that my life had been preserved on purpose. Not because I was exceptional, but because His Word kept unfolding inside me. When God speaks, His promises endure. Darkness cannot edit them. Despair cannot cancel them.

Years earlier, I remembered the night His voice thundered through my room, rich and unshakable.

I AM going to make you great.

Back then, I had no idea what greatness would cost. I could not imagine it would demand the shattering of nearly everything. Yet standing on the far side of a valley I once feared would swallow me whole, I finally understood.

Greatness is not a pedestal.

It is a weight. A responsibility. A mantle.

God was not crafting my brand. He was forging my backbone.

I remembered a prophecy spoken at a conference Brian invited me to, delivered by a pastor who knew nothing about my story.

Thousands are tied to your destiny. The Lord showed me how He keeps breaking you down and building you up.

At the time, it sounded lofty. After the fire, it sounded like truth. God had not been punishing me. He had been shaping me into someone He could trust with His people, His mysteries, His glory.

Sometimes formation looks like devastation. Not because God delights in suffering, because He does not, but because certain callings require depths you cannot learn from sermons or conferences. Some assignments are forged in silence. Some identities are only revealed when everything else gets stripped away.

The wilderness did that. It peeled away every voice but His. Every dependency but Him. Until what He planted was the only thing left standing.

This was my becoming, not the version I expected, not the one others would celebrate, but the becoming authored by God before I ever drew breath.

I was not the woman I had been before the fall. She was gone. I was not the same woman who endured the wilderness. She had fulfilled her assignment. Now I was emerging into someone new, shaped through encounters that tested my spirit and refined my discernment.

The God who walked beside me in my darkest hours was now beckoning me forward. Not back to who I was, but toward the woman I was destined to become.

Becoming did not feel like crossing a finish line. It felt like responding to a summons. A gentle tug in my spirit that sounded like heaven whispering, stand up. It is time.

But before I could step fully into the new, God brought me back through the remnants of my past. Not to reopen wounds, but to reveal what had healed, what had shifted, and what would never bind me again.

One afternoon, I sat on the edge of my bed, eyes fixed on the floor, the same floor where I had once curled up trembling under spiritual assault. I half expected memory to flood me with cold fear, but instead something warm settled over me.

Authority.

Not loud. Not brash. Rooted. Quiet. The kind that comes from surviving nights you thought would never end.

I'm not afraid anymore, I whispered, barely recognizing my own voice.

And it was true.

Fear had been a tyrant I never remember choosing to serve, yet for a long time I did. The darkness tried to convince me it owned me. It whispered that I was ruined, marked, forsaken. But there I was, in the very spot where I had begged God for release, and truth surged inside me like a steady flame.

What tried to kill me taught me who I am.

Not because suffering is noble, but because God was present in every agonizing moment.

I remembered the nights when prayer felt impossible. The days when my thoughts unraveled like fraying thread. The times when I felt creatures beneath my skin and questioned my sanity. In those moments I thought faith was feeling God near.

But the wilderness taught me something deeper.

Faith is the choice to hold onto God when your senses betray you. When your body screams. When your mind threatens to unravel. When emotions collapse under the weight of despair.

Faith is defiance.

And I had lived a year of defiant trust.

As sunlight spilled across the floor, and it dawned upon me, not with thunder or vision, but with steady warmth.

You survived because you are called.

Not called in theory. Called in reality. Called in fire, in warfare, in the crucible of breaking and remaking.

And suddenly I understood why this season had been so violent. What lay ahead demanded a woman who knew God not through ritual or familiarity, but through raw encounter. A woman who could stand before shattered souls and say, I have seen the pit, and God climbs into it with you. A woman who could face darkness without flinching, not because she was fearless by nature, but because she had learned the authority of covenant.

Becoming meant recognizing the battles did not disqualify me. They prepared me.

The pain did not lessen my spirit. It deepened it.

The silence did not leave me abandoned. It anchored me.

The breaking did not annihilate me. It built me.

Then Genesis 2:22 rose in my mind, the verse that pastor had shouted over me like a hammer striking steel.

And the Lord God built the woman.

Not formed. Not shaped. Built.

Constructed piece by piece. Layer by layer. Intentional. Measured. Purposeful.

God was crafting me, not into the woman I dreamed of being, but into the woman He needed me to be. Gratitude spilled out of me before I could stop it.

Thank You for trusting me with the breaking.

Not gratitude for pain, but for what purpose birthed through it. The wilderness had cracked wells inside me so glory could flow. Suffering had forged authority. Shadows had etched depth. Silence had sharpened my hearing.

This was becoming. Not polished. Not perfected. Fully awake.

And the awakening was only beginning.

Becoming required me to revisit the places where my soul had splintered, but this time I returned with eyes that could see. I stepped into my living room one morning, the same space where I had once crawled across the floor gasping for breath while darkness coiled around me like a serpent.

But now the air felt different.

It did not reek of fear. It carried lightness.

My ribs expanded without resistance. I placed my hand on the cool wall and instead of remembering my collapse, I remembered my survival.

Healing is not only the absence of pain.

It is the ability to walk back onto the battlefield and see victory where there used to be devastation.

I inhaled deeply and murmured into the room, I'm still here.

Not fragmented. Not crawling. Not begging for escape.

Here. Standing.

And it hit me that resurrection starts long before a miracle shows up in the natural. It begins quietly in the spirit. It changes you steadily until one day you realize, I am not the same, and I will never be the same.

The first sign of this shift was subtle. I no longer woke bracing for terror. My body stopped flinching at every creak and whisper. A peace settled over me, not forced, not imagined, achingly real.

The peace Paul talked about.

The kind that makes no sense.

The kind that holds you steady even when life is unstable.

It was not denial. It was divine steadiness.

One morning, I woke before dawn. The sky was still dark, just a faint hint of blue teasing the horizon. Normally I would have stayed in bed, hesitant to disturb the quiet. But an inner stirring called me.

I wrapped myself in my blanket and stood by the window.

Like clay in a potter's hands.

Like a seed splitting open to reach the light.

For the first time, I did not resent the breaking. I honored it. Only a broken seed grows. Only a shattered alabaster box releases fragrance. Only a broken woman can carry resurrection in her voice.

Responsibility is not glamorous. It is obedience. It is carrying glory with humility, choosing purity in chaos, loving after betrayal taught you to guard your heart, saying yes when no seems safer.

Becoming meant stepping into that responsibility with a willing heart.

As I journaled one evening, that prophetic night replayed in my mind. The pastor's voice trembling with urgency.

Thousands are tied to your destiny. You will feed multitudes. God showed me how He has been breaking you down and building you up, like Genesis 2:22.

God built the woman.

Back then it sounded poetic. Now it sounded architectural. God had not been reacting to my life. He had been constructing me through it. He was designing me with a blueprint bigger than my pain.

And suddenly I saw them, not with my eyes, but in the Spirit.

Faces.

Thousands.

Men, women, children.

Broken, abandoned, tormented.

Not looking for cute sermons, looking for a lifeline.

They needed presence. Someone who could say, I know what darkness feels like, and I know the God who shatters it.

Becoming was not just healing.

It was transformation.

Pain became catalyst, not prison.

What tried to silence me trained my voice.

What tried to bury my spirit forged resolve.

I closed my journal and whispered the only answer that felt honest.

Yes, Lord. Yes. Whatever You will, my answer is yes.

The following week, a new rhythm settled into me. Steadiness in my legs. Strength in my back. Clarity in my thoughts. I was not merely recovering.

I was rising.

This was not the naive faith of youth.

This was scarred faith.

Tested faith.

Faith with grit.

I had walked through a valley most people refuse to name. A place where doctrine becomes thin and encounter becomes your only shelter.

On the other side of that darkness, I did not just know about God.

I knew Him.

He had been my healer, my defender, my comforter, my strategist.

Some chapters deserve privacy.

But endings deserve peace.

Every resurrection story reaches a moment where the survivor must choose.

Will I return to who I was?

Or will I step forward as who I have become?

One morning, just before sunrise, I felt that crossroads in my bones. The world outside my window was gray, caught between night and morning, and something inside me hovered there too.

Almost reborn.

Not fully realized.

Then the Holy Spirit spoke, wrapping around me like a Father's voice.

Daughter, rise.

Not urgent.

Not harsh.

Gentle.

Certain.

And for the first time since the attacks began, I felt identity settle like foundation. This was not merely recovery.

This was reintroduction.

God was leading me back to myself.

The first change I noticed was my voice.

For months, words had lodged in my throat like stones. Even whispering Scripture felt like backlash. But now I found myself reading aloud in my living room, praying softly in the kitchen, singing worship while washing dishes.

No trembling.

No constriction.

No torment beneath my skin.

My voice was mine again.

Not only restored. Fortified.

I did not sound like the woman before the wilderness.

I sounded like someone who walked through fire and came out carrying weight.

And I finally understood why the enemy fought so hard to silence me.

My voice is a weapon.

Not because it is loud.

Because it speaks truth.

A truth the enemy cannot bear.

God delivers.

Darkness breaks.

Survival is not random. It is sovereign.

I expected my mind would remain fragile even after deliverance. Trauma lingers. It rewires pathways. It leaves ghost impressions of fear.

But something happened that I could not fully explain then.

God rewired my thoughts.

Triggers that once sent me spiraling no longer stirred panic. Memories that had suffocated me felt distant, not denied, disarmed. My mind became a sanctuary.

Not empty.

Peaceful.

This was not natural healing.

It was supernatural reconstruction.

God does not patch the broken places.

He rebuilds the framework.

One day I touched my forehead and whispered, Thank You.

Not for the suffering, but for the clarity that came after it.

For a long time, ministry felt like a distant dream. I could barely stand. How could I stand before others?

Then God drew me back into the river.

First gently, through dreams and nudges.

Then boldly, through invitations and confirmations.

Dr. Smith said something in a session that cracked my chest open.

Your calling never left you. You stepped aside while God operated.

He was right.

The attack did not steal my calling.

It deepened it.

So when the 107 Collective was born, when conferences came to life, South Africa, then Jamaica, I realized I was no longer ministering from pain.

I was ministering from authority.

I preached like someone who stared death down and lived.

I prayed like someone who confronted darkness and watched it retreat.

I worshipped like someone who learned God's voice in silence.

The anointing felt different now.

Not light.

Not bubbly.

Heavy with glory.

Rich with purpose.

People wept, chains snapped, healing moved through rooms like a stream that knows its direction.

And I knew, I was irrevocably changed.

The Final Severing of Shame came quietly.

After one ministry session, I sat alone and realized something with shock.

Shame was gone. Not hidden.

Not managed. Released.

Shame had been the enemy's favorite weapon, not my mistakes, but the whisper that said I was forsaken.

But God had not only forgiven me. He restored me.

The Naomi before the fall was innocent.

The Naomi after the wilderness was anointed.

And there is no shame in anointing.

Forgiveness unfolded in layers.

I did not need to forgive Brian for how our story ended. It simply ended. But I realized I needed to bless him, not out of obligation, but out of freedom.

One night, with moonlight as witness, I whispered.

Lord, bless him. Heal what needs healing. Restore what was lost. Release what was never meant to stay.

When those words left my lips, the last residue lifted like dust.

Becoming meant release.

Clean. Quiet. Complete.

Then purpose finally fit.

One ordinary Tuesday, I sat at my desk editing this book, and it struck me.

The story no longer hurt. The memories were still vivid.

The battles still real.

But the sting was gone.

What once threatened to consume me now breathed life into me, into others, into whoever would read these pages.

I leaned back and let out a sigh that felt like it carried a decade.

And God spoke.

Tell it boldly.

Not timidly. Not wrapped in apologies.

Boldly.

People do not get liberated by sanitized testimonies.

They need the raw truth.

And my truth is simple. I walked through darkness.

God never abandoned me.

That is the story I am called to tell.

The story that will nourish nations and break chains.

This is the story I am still becoming.

Becoming is not a single moment of rising.

It is the realization you have been rising all along.

I understood this in the most unexpected place, my kitchen, barefoot, holding a glass of water.

After a humble prayer, a soft conversation with God about the day ahead, something settled inside me.

Not a tremor.

An anchor.

Peace enveloped me, thick and pure, and my knees nearly buckled.

Clarity struck like sunlight through curtains.

I am whole.

Not healing.

Not recovering.

Whole.

Not a wholeness that denies pain, but one that integrates it, redeems it, and turns it into fuel.

Wholeness that feels like exhaling for the first time in years.

With wholeness came a new gift.

God began to reintroduce me to myself.

Not the girl on Grandma's porch.

Not the woman who fell in love.

Not even the fighter who survived the wilderness.

The prophet. The intercessor. The daughter of fire.

The woman crafted by His hands.

I began to see myself through heaven's eyes, not fragile, not damaged, but entrusted. Chosen. Set apart for a purpose that required storms and still worship.

And I embraced that identity without apology.

Because the mantle of deliverance cannot be taught.

It must be survived.

When it settled on me, it felt like warm oil down my back.

Heavy. Holy. Irrevocable.

From that moment, everything shifted.

When I prayed, atmospheres changed.

When I worshipped, barriers cracked.

When I spoke, people felt God before I finished my sentence.

Not because I was special.

Because I carried evidence.

I was not ministering from theory.

I was ministering from testimony.

God never announces your promotion to the world.

He reveals it to you.

My graduation into purpose did not come with applause.

It arrived in stillness.

One night, I walked into my bedroom, the same room where the wilderness almost swallowed me, and instead of memory pulling me under, authority rose in me like a wall.

I whispered.

Thank You for trusting me with the dark.

Not because darkness had goodness, but because God's faithfulness was undeniable.

That night I asked the question that had lived in me for too long.

Why did You break me so deeply?

And clarity came, not only in words, but in seeing.

Every version of me. The girl. The teenager. The minister.

The intercessor.

The woman who stumbled.

The warrior who clawed her way back.

Each one mattered.

Each one played a part.

But none of them were ready to carry the weight of nations.

So He broke me, not to destroy me, but to reshape me. To give me depth no sermon could teach. Discernment no book could hand me. Compassion only suffering can forge. Power tempered by fire.

When that understanding settled, I breathed a quiet, I understand.

And then the most surprising part.

No bitterness.

No longing.

No nostalgia.

Completion.

God had drawn a line in the sand. The ink had dried. The past had served its purpose. The story was mine now.

Becoming meant stepping forward unburdened.

Not rewriting history.

Releasing it.

Fully. Quietly.

Completely.

The day before I finished this chapter, God whispered something that settled deep.

What you survived was not meant to kill you. It was meant to awaken you.

Awaken me to His voice.

To my authority.

To my calling.

To my identity.

To my purpose.

Awaken me to the truth that I am not the woman I was before.

I am the woman who rose after.

And that rising, that awakening, that transformation, this is what it means to become.

Becoming is not a destination.

It is a rhythm.

A posture.

A continual unfolding.

Each day God reveals another layer of who I am meant to be.

I carry the evidence of deliverance in my voice, my prayers, my presence.

I am here.

I am alive.

I am chosen.

I am becoming, not who the world expects, not who my past predicted, but who God meticulously crafted with His own hands.

And to you, the one reading this story, may you rise too. May you find Him in your wilderness. May you encounter the God who remains, who rebuilds, who resurrects.

If you are breathing, you are not finished.

You are becoming.

SELAH MOMENT

The Final Pause Before Becoming

There comes a point in every journey where the story slows. The dust settles.

And heaven invites you to look back not with shame, not with regret, but with recognition.

A holy pause.

A Selah. If you have reached this page, you have walked with me through valleys and visions, heartbreaks and healings, questions and quiet miracles. You have watched God leave His fingerprints on years that once felt broken, delayed, or forgotten. And now, as we stand together on the threshold between who you were and who you are becoming, I want to give you space not to rush forward, but to breathe.

Because everything you have lived has been shaping you for where you are going.

You are not alone in this transformation.

Your story is ancient.

Your journey echoes Scripture.

Your becoming belongs to a lineage older than time.

So pause here. Let the parallels speak.

- If your life feels like Joseph's...

If you have been betrayed, misunderstood, discarded, or forced into seasons you never chose — Selah.

Joseph's pit was not the end. Neither is yours.

Your dreams are not dead. They are ripening.

- If your heart has walked Esther's path...

If you were hidden, prepared in obscurity, then thrust into assignments larger than your confidence — Selah.

You were made for such a time as this, even when courage trembles in your chest.

- If your soul has cried like Job's...

If you have asked God the hard questions, if you have tasted grief language cannot contain, Selah.

God has been closer than your breath, even when silence felt like abandonment.

Restoration is not a rumor. It is your portion.

- If you have run like Jonah...

If fear made you flee, if shame made you shrink, if obedience felt too heavy — Selah.

The mercy that swallowed Jonah whole is the same mercy carrying you now.

- If you have fought like Joshua...

If you have stood at the edge of promises too big for your strength, staring down fortified walls — Selah.

The land is still yours.

The giants are not greater than the God who goes before you.

    • If you have sung through caves like David...

If your worship was born from wounds, if you were anointed but not yet appointed — Selah.

You are still a king in the making.

Your throne is not at risk.

    • If you have felt forgotten, like Moses...

If you spent years wandering, wondering if you misheard God — Selah.

The burning bush appears when it is time.

Not one day early.

Not one day late. Now look at your own life. Really look.

Your pits and your palaces.

Your storms and your second chances.

Your lions and your loves.

Your victories and your wounds. Every chapter has been shaping a story larger than your pain.

A story God Himself is authoring.

And the same Spirit who carried Joseph, Esther, Job, Jonah, Joshua, David, and Moses is carrying you. Selah.

Let that truth settle into your bones.

Ask yourself gently:

Where did God keep me when I thought I was lost?

What prisons became preparation?

What storms did I survive without realizing He was holding me?

What promises were whispered over my life that I am finally ready to believe again?

What part of my story have I been afraid to own because owning it means stepping into destiny?

Selah.

Breathe.

Listen.

Receive.

A Prayer for the One Who Is Becoming

Heavenly Father, I pray for the person holding this book, for the one standing on the edge of promise, for the one who has walked through fire, wilderness, and wonder. I ask that You wrap them in Your presence, LORD.

Please whisper truths to them in every place that lies echo, just as You whispered to me.

Let the chains of their past fall without ceremony. Let the shame that clung to their name lose its voice.

Let the enemy who tormented them be silenced forever. Let the destiny written over their life rise with new breath. Make them bold. Make them walk in the wholeness that You have won them. Make them unshakeable.

And above all,

Make them yours, in Jesus name.

Amen.

A Final Word Before You Turn the Page

This is your Selah. Your pause at the threshold. Your breath before the becoming.

When you rise from this moment, you do not rise as who you were; you rise as who God always knew you would be.

And the story continues.

Guided Reflection

1. Quiet Invitation

Take a moment. Breathe. Slow your thoughts. Place your hand on your heart.

You have walked through Naomi's journey, but now, this chapter becomes yours.

This is your space to reflect, to release, to remember that God is near.

"Be still and know that I am God." Psalm 46:10

---

2. Reflection Prompts (Answer Slowly)

Write your answers in your own handwriting your story deserves your ink.

Where in your life did you feel like God was absent? *(Describe the moment, the memory, the ache.)*

What lies did the enemy try to make you believe about yourself?

Where can you now see that God was actually protecting or carrying you?

What part of your heart is still healing? *(No shame. No rush.)*

What do you need to release to God today?

3. Identity Declarations (Speak These Out Loud)

Say these slowly. Let them wash over you. Let them rewire what pain tried to teach you.

I am not forgotten. I am beloved. God has not left me. My story is not over. Healing is happening in me, even now. What I survived will not be wasted. I am becoming who God designed me to be.

4. Personal Covenant Statement

Whenever you feel ready you may write your own statement of trust in the lines below:

"Father *God, even when I cannot trace You, I will trust that You are faithful. I surrender my story back to You, in Jesus' name, amen. Write Your glory through my life."*

---

5. Closing Prayer

Lord Jesus,

I place my heart in Your hands. Heal what hurts. Restore what has been broken. Silence every lie, every fear, every shadow. Let Your love settle deep into the places I once hid. Lead me into the fullness of who I am in You. I say yes to becoming. Amen.

This is the day I chose healing.

Signature: _ Date:

CONTINUE THE JOURNEY

3 0-Day Becoming Journey (Reader Bonus)

If this story awakened something in you, I invite you into a 30-day guided encounter with God through reflections, prayers, journaling prompts, and prophetic activations to help you walk out your own becoming.

ABOUT AUTHOR

Latoya Shea is a speaker, teacher, and prophetic intercessor whose life testifies to the relentless love and faithfulness of God. Born in Jamaica and now based in the United States, she has served in ministry, healthcare, and community leadership, helping others encounter the healing presence of Jesus through prayer, teaching, and compassionate service.

Known for her transparency, courage, and unshakeable belief in God's power to restore, Latoya carries a message of hope for those who have walked through trauma, spiritual warfare, and seasons of deep wilderness. Her story is not one of perfection but of **becoming**, through grace.

She lives to remind others that **no matter how dark the night, God's light always guides the way.**

www.ingramcontent.com/pod-product-compliance
Lightning Source LLC
Chambersburg PA
CBHW021200130626
46554CB00005B/1918